R. Paul Caudill

HEBREWS

A Translation with Notes

BROADMAN PRESS

Nashville,

D0813885

Unless otherwise stated, all Scripture quotations are from the American Standard
Version of the Bible.
Scripture quotations marked (AT) are the author's own translation.

Library of Congress Cataloging in Publication Data
Bible.   N.T.   Hebrews.   English.   Caudill.   1985.
    Hebrews: a translation with notes.

    1. Bible.   N.T.   Hebrews—Commentaries.
I. Caudill, R. Paul.   II. Title.
BS2773.C38 1985   227'.870529   84-21415
ISBN 0-8054-1395-2

To the ambassadors of Christ who seek
to understand the relationship of the
Old Testament to the New Testament,
and to proclaim the superiority of
Jesus Christ who is Savior and Lord
of all people who believe in Him.

CONTENTS

PREFACE

In this translation I have endeavored to provide a work with outline, footnotes, and explanatory notes that will enable both the careful and the casual student of the Scriptures to have a helpful workshop in building sermons, devotional messages, or any type of dissertation or dialogue relating to the Epistle to the Hebrews. Unless otherwise noted, all translations of Scripture are mine.

The copious footnotes reflect the varied meanings of the original Greek words in usage. Language is as a growing organism, ever changing both in scope and related meaning, but usually there is an obvious residue of meaning in the current usage of the word in its relation to the root idea of the parent word.

I have used the third edition of *The Greek New Testament* (United Bible Societies, 1975) edited by Aland, Black, Martini, Metzger, and Wikgren as the basis of the translation, together with the texts of Brooke Foss Westcott and Fenton John Anthony Hort (The Macmillan Company, New York, 1929), and Professor Eberhard Nestle (British and Foreign Bible Society, London, 1934). I have endeavored to let the Greek text speak for itself without personal theological bias, and to translate the Greek as literally as possible into contemporary English.

I owe a debt of gratitude to Dr. John B. Polhill, professor of New Testament Interpretation, The Southern Baptist Theological Seminary, for his careful reading of the manuscript and for valuable comments. I owe thanks also to professor Edith Faye Easterling of Florida for her good work as an English critic, and to my gifted secretary, Mrs. Wayne (Eugenia) Price, for her capable work. I owe my great thanks to my wife, Fern, for her patient assistance in the work and for her helpful suggestions.

R. Paul Caudill
October 5, 1984

FOREWORD

Those familiar with R. Paul Caudill's previous translations of Ephesians, Philippians, and 1 Corinthians will welcome this new work on Hebrews. It will prove most useful to the pastor who has had some training in the Greek language, but it is written in such fashion as to be helpful to those with no facility in the original tongue. The format to the book, which is really a minicommentary, consists of a brief introduction which sets the epistle in context. This is followed by Dr. Caudill's own translation of the text which is sufficiently literal to preserve as much as possible the original word order of the Greek text as well as the different nuances of meaning. Very helpful notes are included at the bottom of each page of translation which deal primarily with the range of meaning for the pivotal words in the text. The final section of the book, about half the total text, consists of explanatory notes which give a running commentary on Hebrews.

Paul Caudill has used the best available Greek tools and scholarly works on Hebrews in preparing his translation and commentary. He has presented the fruits of this labor in a highly readable and practical fashion. He majors on those issues which are of concern for the average Christian's understanding of his faith and for his day-to-day living. The pastor who wishes to teach from Hebrews will find in this single volume a useful compendium of the major materials he needs to present the book in a fresh and life-centered manner to his congregation.

JOHN POLHILL

INTRODUCTION

The Epistle to the Hebrews presents the reader with a number of problems which are still unsolved. In this respect, Dr. A. T. Robertson ranked the epistle with "the Fourth Gospel, the Apocalypse of John, and Second Peter."[1] Unanswered is the question as to: the author, the immediate recipients, the place from which the epistle was written, and the exact date of the writing. Nevertheless, the writer leaves no doubt concerning the unique character and the exalted position of the risen Christ. As Savior and Lord, and as the perfect High Priest who made, once and for all, the perfect atoning sacrifice for the remission of sins, He thereby provided all people with the long-awaited faith road of direct access to God.

The Title and Text

Early writers regarded the Book of Hebrews as an epistle.[2] While there is no salutation or address as is commonly found in epistles, the book does close with salutations. The King James Version calls the book "The Epistle of Paul the Apostle to the Hebrews," but most of the oldest manuscripts have "To Hebrews" for the title.

Differing views prevail as to the original text, but internal evidence supports the view that the Greek text is "original and not a translation from any form of Aramaic."[3] This premise is based not only upon the rhetorical characteristics of the book but also upon the style and vocabulary in general. Some hold that the epistle was first written in Hebrew and later translated into Greek, but my position is that the original text was in Greek as we now have it. The style of the epistle as a whole suggests that it belongs to the literary *Koinē* of the time and perhaps surpasses any other New Testament letter when viewed from the standpoint of literary composition. I stand in awe as I contemplate the excellency of the composition of the book and the brilliant cascades of thought that flow so logically in sequence.

The Authorship

Here scholars are again divided, and the question remains unsolved. Some would attribute the authorship to Barnabas, Peter, Priscilla, Silas, Paul, Luke, or Apollos. There is no extant writing by Barnabas with which to compare the style and thought of the epistle. And there is really little to support the view of Harnak, Randall Harris, and G. H. Moulton—the view that Aquila and Priscilla were the joint authors of the epistle. The oldest extant Greek MSS. (Aleph A B) merely have *Pros Hebraious* as the title.[4] The writers in the early centuries offer little help as to authorship since the epistle was at first rejected in the West as a part of the canon. The Book of Hebrews was not generally accepted as a New Testament book until the time of Athanasius in the middle of the fourth century. The Muratorian Canon, which offers the first compilation of New Testament books (circa AD 170), does not so much as mention Hebrews. Cyprian did not mention the book; and Eusebius, early church historian, regarded Hebrews as a disputed book. Neither Calvin nor Luther regarded Paul as the author of the book. However, the Alexandrian school of thought received the book as "Paul's for substance"[5] as did the Eastern Church. But the form, style, and Christology hardly combine to suggest Pauline authorship.[6]

My own position favors that of Hugh Montefiore in the premise that Apollos is the "one person who seems to satisfy all the requirements for authorship."[7] In support of Apollos as author are these facts: he was a Jew (Acts 18:24); a native of Alexandria and, viewed in relation to the works of Philo Judaeus, an eloquent speaker (Acts 18:24); powerful in the Scriptures (Acts 18:24); an accurate teacher (Acts 18:25); instructed in the way of the Lord (Acts 18:25); one who "spoke boldly in the synagogue," was powerful in his confutation of the Jews (Acts 18:28); with reference to the messiahship of Jesus, one who was helpful in "resolving the doubts of Jewish converts to Christianity"; last of all, the author of Acts appeared to be deeply impressed by Apollos while Paul seemed to put Apollos in "the same category as himself and Peter" (1 Cor. 1:12; 3:22).[8] Moreover, the author of Hebrews had what Barclay calls "The double Background."[9] He appeared to be thoroughly acquainted with the thought of the ancient world as reflected by the Greek minds of his day, and out of his Jewish background he set forth the perfect answer to the centuries-old longings of both Hebrew and Greek minds to get away from "shadows" to the fullness of "truth."

The Date

Here again the views of scholars differ widely. Westcott held to a date somewhere between AD 64 and 67. Holtzmann and Harnack preferred a date between 81 and 96. Marcus Dods argued that the Temple was still standing when the epistle was written, as verse 8:13 suggests. Had the Temple service not been still in progress, the words *near disappearance* would hardly be understandable.[10] The mention of Timothy in 13:23 recalls Paul's plea for him to visit him in Rome (2 Tim. 4:11-13). Granted that Timothy came to Rome while Paul was still in prison and was himself put in prison, the years 67-69 seem to offer a probable time for the epistle since Nero's own death occurred on June 8, AD 68; Paul was put to death before that. On the basis of internal evidence, the Christians to whom the epistle was addressed were at least second generation Christians (2:3). Moreover, they were called to look back on their former days (10:32). There is history behind them (13:7). There are references to persecution to date the letter, for some of their former leaders had made the supreme sacrifice (13:7). Though they themselves had not yet resisted unto blood (12:4), they had suffered the plundering of their goods (10:32-34). The risk of future persecutions is also obvious in the letter. We know that there was great persecution of Christians in the time of Nero (AD 64) and also in the time of Domitian, around AD 85.

The Destination

Some scholars have held that the letter was directed to Gentiles, but it is difficult to accept this premise since the entire thought of the epistle is slanted toward the Jewish tradition and concepts of spiritual doctrines. The elaborate apology for the Christian faith set forth in Hebrews seems rather to call for an audience of Jewish background than for one of the pagan or Gentile background.

Furthermore, because of the absence of allusions to heathenisms and the fact that the epistle was addressed to Jewish Christians who were in "great danger from Judaism, and as intimately acquainted with the Jewish ritual," many scholars feel that "these circumstances are more particularly applicable to Jewish Christians residing in Palestine."[11] The word *Hebrew* as used in the New Testament does not necessarily refer to all Jews but rather to those who were more thoroughly of Jewish origin and habits and who spoke the vernacular language of the country. Jews who resided outside Palestine and were more intimately associated with the Greeks and acquainted with the Greek language "were styled Hellenists." The author of the Acts of the apostles (6:1) seems to make this distinction clear. Certainly the temptations to apostatize under the aggressive influence of Judaism would further support Palestine as the destination of the epistle. Obviously, it was addressed to a Christian congregation of Hebrews however large or small "somewhere."[12]

The experiences alluded to in 10:32-34 certainly suggest "a definite church" as the original recipient of the letter,[13] and the church in Jerusalem, so far as sufferings were concerned, fits well in such a category.

The words *they of Italy* (13:24) could refer to those who had come from Italy or those who were then in Italy. Moreover, "They of Italy" may merely refer to the Jewish Christians who had at one time lived in Rome.

Various other destinations have been suggested: Spain, Ephesus, Berea, Ravenna, Colossae, Laodicea, Cyprus, Antioch, Alexandria, Caesarea, and Jamnia.

It would be difficult to hold that the epistle was addressed only to the Jewish element of the Christian church. The warnings concerning extramarital and premarital sexual relationships (Heb. 13:4) seem to refer more naturally to former pagans than to Jewish Christians. Perhaps a better thought would be that the writer had in mind all Christians, maybe in a church of Jews and Gentiles but predominantly Jewish in origin.

Certainly the recipients were people whom the author knew well. He spoke of their generosity (6:10), their persecution (10:32-34; 12:4), their immaturity (5:11 to 6:12), and his hopes to visit them soon (13:19,23).

The Message

Archibald Hunter calls Hebrews "The Epistle of Priesthood."[14]

After dealing at length with the superiority of Christ in relation to angels, to Moses, and to the divinely instituted Mosaic ritual and priesthood, the writer went on to dwell at length on the temporary nature of the Levitical priesthood:

"He treats of the ritual system and its appliances as mere types of an enduring reality: he characterises the whole body of Levitical ordinances and ceremonies as fleshly; and through all runs the one, sad note, accentuated again and again, 'they can never take away sins:' 'they can never make the comers thereunto perfect:' 'they are mere ordinances of the flesh, imposed until the time of reformation.'"[15]

This concept of Christ as the superior high priest (*archiereus*) pervades the entire epistle just as does the concept of Christ as God's Son. The Levitical priest, who on the day of atonement annually entered the holy of holies, was not allowed to remain long in the sacred chamber; for there was always the consciousness, in the Jewish background, of the danger in approaching God. "No man shall see my face and live" (Ex. 33:20, AT).

Moreover, the high priest had to offer sacrifice first for his own sins and then for the sins of the people. But the sacrifice was not a lasting thing, for the covenant relationship between the Hebrew and God was broken when the Hebrew failed to keep the law. "To break the law was sin, and sin interrupted the access to God, put up a barrier which stopped the way to God."[16] The Levitical sacrifice offered a provisional way to overcome the barriers erected by the breaking of the law, but the sacrifices still had to go on from year to year.

Jesus, the perfect priest, made one sacrifice forever, and that for all who would come to Him by faith. At last, in Jesus Christ, people could see the very face of God. By means of His atoning death, a special relationship came to exist between the believer and the people of God, a relationship that endures and knows no end. In Christ the legal economy of the Mosaic ritual came to an abrupt end. However, the shadows of reality for which the Greek world so long had yearned and for which the Hebrews themselves, in their yearning for the advent of the Messiah, found perfect reality. Note that in the Epistle to the Hebrews, there appears to be no explicit reference to Christ's resurrection though 13:20 may be regarded as an allusion to it.[17] Neither is the crucifixion alluded to. The concluding emphasis is upon Christ's presence in heaven as He sits (not stands as do others of the heavenly host) on the right hand of God in His continuing ministry.

The Purpose

Here again commentators vary in their interpretation of the purpose of the epistle. A. T. Robertson held that "in Hebrews the author is battling to stop a stampede from Christ back to Judaism, a revolt (apostasy) in truth from the living God."[18] It is true that the Judaizers wanted "to make Jews out of Gentile Christians and to fasten Judaism upon Christianity with a purely sacramental type of religion as the result,"[19] but the heart of the purpose of the writer seems to rest upon "the Glory of Jesus as superior at every point to all that Judaism had, as God's Son and man's Saviour, the crown and glory of the Old Testament prophecy, the hope of mankind."[20]

The writer showed great concern for the lack of enthusiasm, the problem of religious drift, "and the loss of courage and zeal on the part of this primitive Christian congregation."[21] Some of the causes for this drift lay in severe persecution and "the delay of the 'Parousia.'"[22] Some of the early believers had become disillusioned while others gave way to ethical compromise and a feeling that they could still identify with Christ even though they conformed to pagan life-styles.[23]

There was also the matter of religious syncretism which cast its threatening shadow over the Christian community by way of the influence of the Essene sacerdotal ideas. Perhaps this is why the author went to such great length "to demonstrate that everything, which was true to the Old Testament pattern, was completely fulfilled and superseded in Jesus Christ—the Son of God, the royal Servant, and the great, eternal High Priest."[24]

Certainly, the writer broke fresh ground and took a "bold stand" in his discussion of the person of Christ, and His superiority to angels and to the prophets of the Old Testament. As God's Son, and as God's agent in the matter of creation (Phil. 2:5-11; Col. 1:13-20; John 1:1-18), the writer drove to the heart of the matter and, with surpassing logic, showed that "Jesus is like Melchizedek and so superior to Aaron (4:14-7:28), works under a better covenant of grace (8:1-13), works in a better sanctuary which is in heaven (9:1-12), offers a better sacrifice which is his own blood (9:13-10:18), and gives us better promises for the fulfillment of his task (10:19-12:3)."[25] Whether or not the chief danger to the Hebrews was a relapse into Judaism, there lay before them the threat of "a loss of the significance of their Christian profession due to their continuing to live under the shadow of Jewish legalism."[26]

At bottom, I agree with Hobbs in saying, "The crusading call of the author is not 'Don't go back!'—but 'Let us go on!' (6:1)."[27] Whatever the age, whatever the circumstance, the redeemed people of God are to declare the gospel to the lost world.

In at least five places in the epistle, the writer challenged his readers to action in the light of their mission (2:1 *ff.*; 3:7 *ff.*; 6:1 *ff.*; 10:19 *ff.*; 12:1 *ff.*).[28]

The real *rest* that beckons to followers of Jesus Christ in every age is the ultimate rest that comes to the believer in heaven. The salvation and adoption unto sonship that comes to believers when they receive Jesus Christ as Savior and Lord and begin their pilgrimage under salvation's rainbow of hope while on earth point to the ultimate realization of salvation in Christ at the last Day. With that realization and all of its glorious aspects, nothing on earth can compare.

Notes

1. A. T. Robertson, *Word Pictures in the New Testament,* vol. 5 (Nashville, Tenn.: Sunday School Board of the SBC, 1932), p. 327.
2. Brooke Foss Westcott, *The Epistle to the Hebrews: The Greek Text with Notes and Essays* (New York: Macmillan and Company, 1889), p. xxix.
3. Ibid., p. xxxiv.
4. Robertson, p. 329.
5. Francis S. Sampson, *A Critical Commentary on the Epistle to the Hebrews* (New York: Robert Carter and Brothers, 1857), p. 29.
6. *The Interpreter's Dictionary of the Bible*, vol. 2 (Nashville, Tenn.: Abingdon Press, 1962), p. 571.
7. Hugh Montefiore, *A Commentary on the Epistle to the Hebrews* (New York: Harper and Row, 1964), p. 9.
8. Ibid., p. 11.
9. William Barclay, *The Letter to the Hebrews* (Philadelphia: The Westminster Press, 1957), p. xiv.
10. Robertson, p. 330.
11. Sampson, p. 28.
12. Herschel H. Hobbs, *Studies in Hebrews* (Nashville, Tenn.: Sunday School Board, Southern Baptist Convention, 1954). p. 7.
13. Robertson, p. 330.
14. Archibald M. Hunter, *Introducing the New Testament* (Philadelphia: The Westminster Press, 1972), p. 90.
15. Marvin R. Vincent, *Word Studies in the New Testament,* vol. 4 (Grand Rapids, Mich.: William B. Eerdmans Publishing Company, 1946), p. 364 *ff.*
16. Barclay, p. xvi.
17. *The Interpreter's Dictionary of the Bible*, p. 574.
18. Robertson, p. 331.
19. Ibid.
20. Ibid.
21. *The Broadman Bible Commentary*, vol. 12 (Nashville, Tenn.: Broadman Press, 1972), p. 9.
22. Ibid., p. 10.
23. Ibid., p. 11.
24. Ibid., p. 12.
25. Robertson, p. 327 *ff.*

26. Hobbs, p. 8.
27. Ibid., p. 11
28. Ibid., p. 9.

Sources Mentioned in Notes on Translation

Bauer—*A Greek-English Lexicon of the New Testament* (Chicago: University of Chicago Press, 1979).

Caudill—*Philippians: A Translation with Notes* (Boone, N.C.: Blue Ridge Press of Boone, Inc., 1980).

Moffatt—*Epistle to the Hebrews,* International Critical Commentary (Edinburgh: P. & P. Clark, 1924).

Polhill—Personal correspondence with Dr. John B. Polhill, The Southern Baptist Theological Seminary.

Robertson—*Word Pictures in the New Testament,* vol. 5 (Nashville, Tenn.: Sunday School Board, SBC, 1931).

Souter—*A Pocket Lexicon to the Greek New Testament* (Oxford University Press, 1943).

Thayer—*Greek-English Lexicon of the New Testament* (Grand Rapids, Mich.: Baker Book House, 1977).

Westcott—*The Epistle to the Hebrews: The Greek Text with Notes and Essays* (New York: MacMillan and Company, 1889).

*Gerhard Kittel, *Theological Dictionary of the New Testament* (Grand Rapids, Mich.: William B. Eerdmans Publishing Company, 1981).

ANALYSIS OF THE EPISTLE

CHAPTER 1

I. God's Final Revelation in His Son (1:1-2a)

1 In many portions and in many ways,[1] God long ago having spoken to the fathers[2] in the prophets,
2 at the last of these days spoke to us in (His) Son whom He made heir of all things,

II. The Character and Power of His Son (1:2b-3)

through whom[3] also He made the worlds;
3 who being the radiance[4] of His glory and the inherent character[5] of His actual being, who sustains all things by the word of His power;

---

1. *polumerōs . . . polutropōs*—"In fragmentary and varied fashion" *(New English Bible).*
2. *tois patrasin*—A general reference to Old Testament "worthies" (Robertson).
3. *di'hou*—Through whom, that is the Son both Heir and Intermediate Agent in the creation of the world. See Colossians 1:16 ff.
4. *apaugasma*—Reflection, effulgence, radiant splendor.
5. *charaktēr*—Originally the engraver's tool which came to mean the "impress" or "mark" made with the tool, and later any "distinguishing peculiarity." Hence, the idea "an exact reproduction."

having brought about purification[6] from sins, He took His seat on the right hand[7] of the Majesty on high;

III. Jesus' Superiority Over Angels (1:4-14)

4   having become by so much better[8] than the angels, inasmuch as He has inherited a name more excellent[9] than they.

5   For to which of the angels[10] did He ever say,
        Thou art my Son,
        I this day have begotten Thee?
    And again,
        I will be to Him as a Father,
        And He shall be to me as a Son?[11]

6   And again,[12] when He shall have brought the firstborn into the world, He says
        And all the angels of God are to worship[13] Him.

7   And with reference to the angels He says,

---

6. *katharismon*—A ceremonial Hellenistic word from a word meaning "to cleanse," hence the sense of "cleansing from sin."

7. *dexiai*—Right as opposed to left. Here as an indication of friendship, trust, and power as God's Son.

8. *kreittōn*—A recurring word setting forth the superiority of Jesus as the Messiah: better covenant, better promises, etc.

9. *diaphorōteron*—A word reflecting difference in the sense of excellency. In degree more outstanding.

10. *aggelōn*—Angels, referred to in general as messengers, envoys, supernatural messengers as here, sons of God, but only Jesus is called God's Son.

11. *patera . . . huion*—See Psalm 2:7 and 2 Samuel 7:14.

12. *palin*—Either a reference to the second coming (as in 9:28) or to the incarnation, depending upon the relationship of *palin* to *eisagagēi*.

13. *proskunēsatōsan autōi*—Worship "in the full sense of worship, not mere reverence or courtesy" (Robertson).

The One who makes His angels winds,[14]
And His servants a flame of fire;

8   but with reference to the Son,
Thy throne,[15] O God, is for ever and ever,
and the scepter of righteousness *is the*
Scepter of Thy kingdom.

9   Thou hast loved righteousness[16] and hated lawlessness;
Therefore God, Thy God, anointed[17] Thee
With the oil of gladness beyond[18] Thy comrades.

10   And,

Thou, in the beginning, Lord, laid the foundation[19] of the earth,
And the heavens are the works of Thy hands;

11   They will perish, but Thou remainest,[20]
And all, as a garment, shall become old,

12   And Thou wilt roll them up as a cloak,

---

14. *pneumata*—From *pneūma*, an old word with varied meanings like breathing, but also (life-) spirit, the soul, without which the body has no life. God's authority over His angels is complete. If He desires to "reduce angels to the elemental forces of wind and fire," as Moffatt holds, that is His privilege. And this is the point of the passage.

15. *ho thronos*—This construction here allows, "God is thy throne" or "Thy throne is God."

16. *dikaiosunēn*—A word that reflects just and upright character on the part of persons. Used of the justice and uprightness of a judge. Here and elsewhere in the New Testament it means "righteousness, uprightness," in the sense of what God requires of us. Used of fulfillment of God's commands and as "the compelling motive" in the conduct of the Christian's life.

17. *echrisen se*—See Isaiah 61:1,3.

18. *para*—Beyond, above, with the idea of comparison.

19. *ethemeliōsas*—Thou . . . laid the foundation. An old word that means also "to found" as of taking the initial steps in building something, or in the establishment of something.

20. *diameneis*—Remainest, as Creator and Preserver of the universe. Christ's existence is eternal.

And as a garment they shall be changed;
but Thou art the same,
And Thy years will not come to an end.[21]

13   But to which of His angels did He ever say,
Sit at my right hand[22]
Until I make thy enemies a footstool of thy feet?

14   Are not all the ministering spirits sent out for service for the sake of
those who are going to inherit salvation?[23]

---

21. *ouk ekleipsousin*—To fail, die out, give out, be eclipsed, die.
22. *ek dexiōn*—Right, as opposed to left. From my right or, as we would say, "on
my right hand" or "at my right hand."
23. *sōtērian*—Salvation used here in the sense of our *final deliverance*. Used
here "of the final salvation in its consummation" (Robertson).

CHAPTER 2

IV. The Great Salvation (2:1-4)

1   Therefore we ought to pay far more attention[1] to the things that were heard lest at any time we be swept away (washed away)[2] *from them.*

2   For if the word spoken through the angels was valid, and every transgression[3] and disobedience received a just[4] penalty,

3   how shall we escape, having neglected[5] so great salvation; which, having first been spoken through the Lord, was confirmed[6] to us by those who heard,

4   God also joining with them at the same time in giving additional testimony both by signs and wonders and by various kinds of powers and by distributions[7] of the Holy Spirit according to His own will?

---

1. *perissoterōs prosechein*—Pay far more attention to, from *prosechō*, to give heed to, follow, pay attention to, be concerned about, notice, care for, apply oneself to.

2. *pararuōmen*—From an old verb (*pararreō*, 2nd aor. pass. subj.), to glide by, flow (as a river) by or past. In passive voice, "be washed away," etc. Only here in the New Testament.

3. *parabasis*—Transgression, overstepping, "violation of the law" (Bauer).

4. *endikon*—Just, deserved, "based on what is right" (Bauer).

5. *amelēsantes*—From *ameleō*, be unconcerned, neglect something or someone, be careless of, not to care for.

6. *ebebaiōthē*—Was confirmed—from *bebaios* meaning stable, here in the sense of established, make firm, strengthen, confirm.

7. *merismois*—Separation, division, apportionment, distribution.

V. A Solemn Warning (2:5-18)

5   For not unto angels did He subject[8] the world to come of which we speak
6   but someone somewhere bore solemn witness saying,

> What is man that Thou shouldest care for him, or the son of man[9]
>
> that thou shouldest visit Him?

7   Thou hast made Him, for a short time,[10] a little lower than the angels, and having crowned Him with glory and honor.
8   Thou hast subordinated[11] all things under His feet.

For in subordinating all things [to Him], He left nothing that was not made subject to Him. But now we see not yet all things subjected to Him;

9   but we do see Jesus, the one who for a little while was made a little lower[12] than the angels because of the suffering of death, crowned with glory and honor, so that by the grace of God He should taste death in behalf of every one.
10   For it was fitting[13] for Him, for whom are all things and through whom are all things, the one who brought many sons unto glory, to

---

8. *hupetaxen*—From *hupotasso,* to make subordinate, or subject something or someone.

9. *huios anthrōpou*—Son of man. Earthly son of earthly man, not a messianic reference in the original Psalm, though, applied by the writer of Hebrews to Christ rather than to mankind in general (Polhill). Literally, "son of man," as often in Ezekiel.

10. *brachu*—From *brachus,* an adjective meaning "little, short"—of time, "for a short time" as here (Bauer).

11. *hupetaxas*—To put in subjection, subject, arrange under, subordinate. See verse five for similar idea.

12. *ēlattōmenon*—From *elattoō,* to make inferior, lower. In the intransitive sense, diminish.

13. *eprepen*—From *prepō,* to be suitable, fitting, or seemly. Imperfect active voice.

make perfect[14] the founder of their salvation through sufferings.

11 For both the One who sanctifies and those being sanctified are all of one;[15] because of which He is not ashamed to call them brothers,

12 saying,

I will proclaim[16] Thy name to My brothers,
In the midst of the congregation I will praise Thee in song;

13 And again,

I will put my trust[17] in Him;

And again,

Behold, I and the children[18] whom God has given Me.

14 Since therefore the children have shared in blood and flesh, He also Himself likewise shared the same things with them, so that by means of His death He might bring to naught[19] him that has the power of death, that is, the devil,

15 and that He might set free[20] those who, in fear of death throughout all their lifetime, were subject to slavery.

---

14. *teleiōsai*—Finish, complete, to bring to the goal, or to an end, to the full measure, to perfection. The idea here deals with the humanity of Jesus. He lived a human life that He might be able to sympathize with His people and become an "effective leader in the work of salvation" (Robertson).

15. *ex henos*—Of One, that is God. The writer has in mind here the "whole company of Christ," the one body who are His people, and they are all of the same God and Father in their spiritual state.

16. *apaggelō*—To tell, report, announce, proclaim, declare, confess.

17. *pepoithōs*—From *peithō*, a verb meaning in the active voice to convince, persuade; but in the passive sense, as here, believe, come to believe, be convinced, persuaded.

18. *ta paidia*—The children—a tender, beautiful reference to the children of God, called sons *(huioi)*.

19. *katargēsei*—Make powerless, idle, ineffective, set aside, wipe out, abolish.

20. *apallaxēi*—From *appallassō*, to set free from, deliver, release, free.

16   For surely it is not angels that He is helping but the descendants[21] of
          Abraham that He is helping.

17   For which reason He (Jesus) was under obligation[22] to be made like
          unto His brothers in every respect, that He might become a merciful
          and faithful High Priest in things relating to God, so as to atone for
          the sins of the people.

18   For in that He Himself has suffered, being tempted,[23] He is able to
          run to the cry[24] of those who are being tempted.

---

21. *spermatos*—In nature, the seeds of plants or the male seed, descendants,
     posterity, children. Here "the spiritual Israel (Gal. 3:29)" (Robertson),
     "children of faith" (Rom. 9:7).

22. *ōpheilen*—From *opheilō,* an old word meaning "in its ordinary sense"
     (Moulton and Milligan), to be bound by necessity or under obligation to do
     something.

23. *peirazomenois*—From *peirazō,* to try, make trial of, put to the test, as by
     Satan (Matt. 4:8-11).

24. *boēthēsai*—From *boē,* a cry, and *theō,* to run.

CHAPTER 3

VI. Jesus, Superior to Moses (3:1-6)

1   Therefore, holy[1] brothers, sharers of a heavenly calling, fix[2] your mind on Jesus, the Apostle and High Priest of our confession,

2   who was faithful[3] unto Him that appointed Him even as was Moses in all His (God's) house.

3   For this One (Jesus) has been considered worthy[4] of more glory[5] than

---

1. **hagioi**—Holy, sacred, consecrated, dedicated to God, set apart completely unto God for His service. "The word is used of one who is consecrated and worthy of veneration; used of sacrifices and offerings prepared for God with solemn rite; in a moral sense, *pure, sinless, upright;* used in the New Testament of those whose lives are set apart for or unto God, to be exclusively his; hence, *saints"* (Caudill, *Philippians*).

2. **katanoēsate**—Observe (carefully), notice, consider, contemplate, look at (with reflection) (Bauer). Here, in a spiritual sense. Hence, "fix your mind on Jesus."

3. **piston**—Dependable, trustworthy, worthy of confidence. In active sense, trusting, full of faith, believing, faithful.

4. **ēxiōtai**—From **axioō** (perfect passive indicative), to consider deserving, worthy, suitable, fitting.

5. **doxēs**—"*The unspoken manifestation of God;* the Shekinah (in Jewish theology, the divine presence); *honor, praise, glory, splendor, excellence, etc."* (Caudill, *Philippians*).

Moses by so much as he who built and furnished the house has more honor than the house itself.

4   For every house is built and furnished by someone, but the One who built and furnished all things[6] is God.

5   And Moses indeed was faithful in all His *(God's)* house as a servant,[7] for a testimony[8] of the things to be spoken later,

6   but Christ as a Son over His house; whose house we are, if indeed we hold fast[9] our confidence and the pride of our hope.

VII. God's Rest for His People (3:7 to 4:13)

7   Therefore just as the Holy Spirit says,
     Today if you should hear[10] His voice,

8   Harden[11] not your hearts as in the rebellion,[12]
     Like the day of the testng in the wilderness

9   Where your fathers tempted Me by testing[13] Me
     And saw My works forty years;

---

6. *panta*—All things. "God is the Creator of all things and so of his 'house' which his Son, Jesus Christ, founded and supervises" (Robertson).

7. *therapōn*—A slave, servant, related to the verb *therapeuō*, to heal, to serve . . . and to the word *therapeia*, service, care, serving.

8. *marturion*—Proof, testimony, a spoken or written testimony that serves as proof of something.

9. *kataschōmen*—From *katechō*, hinder, hold back, as to prevent someone from going away, depress, hold down, check, restrain, hold fast, retain.

10. *ean tēs phōnēs autou akousēte*—That is, if you hear His voice *with understanding.* Another note of warning against apostasy.

11. *sklērunēte*—Harden a thing, meaning also to "stiffen the neck." Passive idea: become or be hardened.

12. *parapikrasmōi*—Irritation, provocation, embitterment; hence, revolt, or rebellion against God (Bauer).

13. *en dokimasiai*—Examination, testing, put to the test, as here.

10   For this reason, I was angry[14] with this generation
          And said, they always go astray[15] in the heart;
          And they did not understand My ways.
11   As I swore in My wrath,
          they shall certainly not enter into My rest.[16]
12   Take care,[17] brothers, lest at any time there shall be in any of you an
      evil heart of disbelief[18] in the falling away[19] from the living God,
13   but rather encourage[20] one another daily, so long as it is called
      today, that none of you be hardened by the deceitfulness of sin;
14   for we have become sharers[21] of the Christ if indeed we hold fast our

---

14. *prosōchthisa*—A compound word from *prosochthizō*, be offended, angry, provoked as with a person or something. A word used "for extreme anger and disgust" (Robertson).

15. *planōntai*—Present middle indicative of *planaō*, be misled, go astray, wander about; in act. voice, lead away, cause to wander, deceive, mislead. Used of those who have strayed away from the ways of God.

16. *katapausin*—Rest, as the sabbath is a day of rest, place of rest. Used here of the rest in Canaan and consequently of "the heavenly rest in which God dwells" (Robertson).

17. *blepete*—From *blepō*, used of eye activity as in Matthew 7:3. We say, "Look out!" in warning one of danger. Be on the lookout, take care, regard, notice, beware of, etc.

18. *apistias*—The opposite of belief, hence, disbelief, or the abject refusal to believe.

19. *en tōi apostēnai*—From *aphistēmi*, here in the sense of withdrawing from, going away, literally, "to stand off from, to step aside from" (Robertson).

20. *parakaleite*—From *parakaleō*, to summons, call to one side, urge, appeal to, exhort, implore, entreat, cheer up, encourage, comfort.

21. *metochoi*—From *metochos*, participating in or sharing with someone as in a heavenly calling (Heb. 3:1).

original confidence[22] until the end,

15   while it is said,

>   Today, if you should hear His voice,[23] may you not harden your
>   hearts as in the rebellion.

16   For who, having heard, became rebellious?[24] Was it not all of those
who came out of Egypt under Moses' leadership?

17   And with whom was He provoked[25] forty years? Was it not with them
that sinned, whose bodies fell in the wilderness?

18   And to whom did He swear that they should not enter into[26] His rest if
not to them who were disobedient?

19   So we see that they were not able to enter because of unbelief.[27]

---

22.   *tēn archēn tēs hupostaseōs*—Literally the beginning of our confidence. A
reference to "faltering believers" such as we have in our churches today when
believers start out "with loud confidence and profession of loyalty" only to
denigrate their profession by backsliding.

23.   *phōnēs autou akousēte*—Here His voice, that is *with understanding* as in
verse 7.

24.   *parepikranan*—See verse 8.

25.   *prosōchthisen*—Same word used for anger in verse 10.

26.   *mē eiseleusesthai eis*—Not enter into. The reference here, of course, is to
Canaan, not heaven.

27.   *apistian*—See verse 12 for similar use of the word *disbelief*.

CHAPTER 4

1   Let us therefore be fearful[1] lest at any time, a promise being left[2] to enter into His rest, some one of you should appear to have come short of it.

2   For we also have had the good news[3] preached to us, just as they; but the word heard did not benefit them, not having been united[4] by faith with them that heard.

3   For we who believed[5] do keep on entering into [the] rest just as He has said,

---

1. *phobēthōmen*—From *phobeō,* be afraid, at times in the sense of being frightened, fear of something or someone, but used also in the sense of respect or reverence for God.

2. *kataleipomenēs*—From *kataleipō,* leave behind, as a person when one leaves a place or leaves others behind as in dying. God's promise to the Israelites still holds for us, notwithstanding their failure.

3. *esmen euēggelismenoi*—From an old word *euaggelion,* glad tidings, or good news. Used here in the sense of bringing good news—the original sense of the verb.

4. *sugkekerasmenous*—From *sugkerannumi,* unite, blend, mix (together). A difficult phrase, as Robertson notes, because of the participial ending. Nevertheless, one thing is certain: those hearing the good news must exercise faith, if it is to have meaning for them.

5. *pisteusantes*—From *pisteuō,* put one's trust in God or the Messiah, believe in, believe on, "cast self upon" God or the Messiah as Savior, Redeemer, and Cleanser from sin.

As I swore in My wrath
They shall certainly not enter into My rest,
although the works were finished from the foundation[6] of the world.

4   For He has spoken somewhere in this way concerning the seventh day, And God rested[7] on the seventh day from all His works;
5   and in this *place* again:[8]
They shall certainly not enter into My rest.
6   Since therefore it remains[9] for some to enter into it, and the former ones having the glad tidings proclaimed to them entered not because of disobedience,
7   again He sets[10] a certain day, Today, by David saying, after so long a time just as it has been said before,
Today if[11] you should hear His voice,
harden not your hearts.
8   For if Joshua had given them rest, He (God) would not be speaking later of another day.[12]
9   Consequently, there remains a sabbath rest[13] for the people of God;

---

6. **katabolēs**—Foundation, beginning, used for casting down (sowing) seed upon the ground or the laying of a foundation for a house.

7. **katepausen**—From **katapauō**, intransitive sense: bring something to an end, stop, restrain, bring to rest; intr. rest, stop, as to stop from work.

8. **palin**—A reference to the passage already quoted in verse 3 and 3:11.

9. **apoleipetai**—From **apoleipō** meaning to remain over or leave behind. A reference to the leftover promise of God which the Israelites, under Moses, failed to make use of.

10. **horizei**—From **horizō**, from **horos**, limit or boundary. Hence, to define, to mark out, determine, appoint, horizon off. See our word *horizon*.

11. **ean**—If. One may hear the proclamation of the Word, but unless there is a response to the hearing, it is without avail.

12. **allēs** . . . **hēmeras**—Another day here refers to the sabbath rest that always awaits all the people of God who hear His voice and harden not their hearts.

13. **sabbatismos**—Sabbath rest, sabbath observance (Bauer). From **sabbatizō** (Ex. 16:30) "to keep the sabbath" and parallels **katapausin** in verse 3.

10   for he who has entered into His rest has himself also rested from his works just as God[14] did from His own.

11   Let us therefore make every effort[15] to enter into that rest lest someone fall in the same pattern of disobedience.

12   For the word of God is living,[16] and energetic,[17] and sharper than any two-edged sword, and piercing[18] as far as the separation of soul and spirit, of both joints and marrow, and is able to judge[19] the thoughts and intents of the heart;

13   and no creature is hidden in His sight, but all things are naked and laid bare[20] to the eyes of Him with whom the accounting is for us.

VIII. The Great High Priest (4:14 to 5:10)

14   Having therefore a great High Priest who has passed through[21] the

---

14. *hōsper . . . Theos*—Just as God did. "The writer pictures salvation as God's rest which man is to share" (Dods, from Robertson, *Word Pictures*).

15. *spoudasōmen*—From *spoudazō,* hurry, hasten, take pains, be zealous or eager.

16. *zōn*—From *zaō,* live, as of physical life over against death. Used also "of the supernatural life of the child of God . . . in the sense of a higher type of life than the animal" (Bauer).

17. *energēs*—Powerful, energetic. We get our word *energy* from this word.

18. *diïknoumenos*—From *diïkneomai,* penetrate, pierce, go through.

19. *kritikos*—Able to judge, discern, as here "the thoughts and intents of the heart."

20. *gumna kai tetrachēlismena*—Bare, naked, stripped, without outer garment, hence open and laid bare *(tetrachēlismena)* from *trachēlizō,* meaning "to bend back the neck" (Robertson) or twist the neck. Hence, everything is open and laid bare to the eyes of Him to whom we must give account.

21. *dielēluthota*—Perfect active participle of *dierchomai,* hence a state of completion. "Jesus has passed through the upper heavens up to the throne of God (1:3) where he performs his function as our high priest" (Robertson).

heavens, Jesus, the Son of God, let us keep on clinging tenaciously[22] to our confession.

15   For we have not a High Priest who is unable to sympathize[23] with our weaknesses, but One who has been tempted in every respect in quite the same way *as we, yet without sin.*[24]

16   Let us therefore keep on coming with boldness to the throne of the grace that we may receive mercy and find grace[25] for timely help.

---

22. *kratōmen*—Present active (volitive) subjunctive of *krateō* used with the genitive case "to cling to tenaciously." Hence, "let us keep on clinging tenaciously to."

23. *sumpathēsai*—Aorist passive infinitive of *sumpatheō*, from old word meaning "to suffer with, sympathize with."

24. *chōris hamartias*—Without sin. Herein lies the difference between Jesus and us. He did no sin, never yielded to sin, and yet in His human life He suffered with us, being tempted as we.

25. *charin*—From *charis*, "A word that in early Greek literature had variant meanings of *gracefulness, gratitude, a favor.* Here the idea seems to be that of a *lovely, unmerited, God-given* experience of his favoring presence felt in the life of man" (Caudill, *Philippians*, p. 24).

CHAPTER 5

1   For every high priest[1] chosen from among men is appointed[2] in behalf of men in things relating to God that he may continually offer[3] both gifts and sacrifices for sins,

2   being able to deal gently with the ignorant and erring ones since He Himself also is beset[4] with weakness,

3   and because of it He is obligated,[5] just as for the people, so also for Himself, to offer *sacrifice* for sins.

4   And no one obtains the honor for himself,[6] rather being called by

---

1. *archiereus*—High priest, Sanhedrin president, used also of Christ who became the Lamb of God offered for the sins of all who would look to Him by faith.

2. *kathistatai*—From *kathistēmi*, ordained, put in charge, appointed, etc.

3. *prospherēi*—From *propherō*, bring, as something to someone, offer, present offerings. A continuous, never-ending mission for the priests "taken from among men."

4. *perikeitai*—From *perikeimai*, lie around or be placed around as a necklace about the neck. Used "of a crowd of people surrounding someone" (Bauer). Hence, beset with weakness.

5. *opheilei*—From *opheilō*, be indebted, owe, as something to someone, obligated as where there is a debt to pay.

6. *heautōi . . . tēn timēn*—The honor for Himself. The office is not for Him as an honor, or as a channel of personal benefit.

God[7] just as Aaron also *was*.

5   So also the Christ glorified[8] not Himself to be made a High Priest,
     but the One who said to Him,
>   Thou art My Son,
>   I today have begotten Thee;
6   as also in another *place* He says,
>   Thou art a priest forever,[9]
>   According to the order of Melchizedek.[10]
7   Who, in the days of His flesh,[11] having offered up both prayers and
     supplications, with strong crying and tears, unto Him that was able
     to deliver Him out of death, and having been heard because of His
     reverence *for God*,
8   although being a Son, He learned obedience[12] by the things which
     He suffered;
9   and having been made perfect[13] He became to all those who obey

---

7. *kaloumenos hupo tou Theou*—Called by God, as every minster of the
   gospel should be.
8. *edoxasen*—From *doxazō*, honor, magnify, glorify, clothe in splendor,
   acknowledge the glory of God.
9. *hiereus eis ton aiōna*—A priest forever, that is, Jesus. Not a temporary
   appointment, as of the priests taken from among men, but an eternal role as
   High Priest.
10. *kata tēn taxin Melchisedek*—Melchizedek appeared only once in the role
    as priest, so Christ offered Himself but once, and that as King and Priest.
11. *sarkos*—From *sarx*, literally, "of the material that covers the bones of a
    human or animal body." The mortal or human nature, the human body itself,
    corporality, the external side of life, and the source of the natural urges of life.
    Jesus was human as well as divine.
12. *hupakoēn*—From *hupakoē*, obedience, used in the New Testament
    especially with reference to obedience to God and to His commands.
13. *teleiōtheis*—From *teleioō*, bring to an end, finish, complete, fulfill (of
    prophecies), bring to full measure. Everything relating to the initial stage of
    Christ's priestly role and kingship as Messiah had been accomplished.
    Nothing was lacking.

Him the cause of eternal salvation,

10   named[14] by God High Priest according to the order of Melchizedek.

IX. Warnings Against Desertion (5:11 to 6:12)

11   Concerning which there is much for us to say, and difficult to explain,[15] since you have become sluggish in hearing.[16]

12   For when, by reason of time you ought to be teachers, you again have need for someone to teach you the basic elements of the elementary principles[17] of God's word, and you have become in need of milk [and] not solid food.

13   For whoever continues to partake of milk is unacquainted[18] with the word of righteousness, for he is a baby;

14   but the solid food is for mature[19] persons, for those having had their faculties trained through exercise to the point of distinguishing[20] both good and evil.

---

14. *prosagoreutheis*—From *prosagoreuō*, designate, call, name.

15. *dusermēneutos*—A verbal compound adjective meaning hard to interpret, hard to explain, hard to make clear to one's understanding.

16. *nōthroi*—From *nōthros*, an adjective that means dull or blunt, and in a spiritual sense sluggish, lazy, slack, remiss. Hence, hard of hearing.

17. *ta stoicheia*—From *stoicheion*, an elementary rule, rudimentary principle, rudiment, fundamental elements or principles of learning. Used also of elemental substances.

18. *apeiros*—From *peira* (a trial, attempt, experiment, essay). Hence, inexperience in a given matter, unacquainted with a given situation or matter. Without experience. Hence, unacquainted with the teachings about righteousness.

19. *teleiōn*—Mature persons, full grown, in contrast to babes or children (1 Cor. 3:1; 13:11; Phil. 3:15).

20. *diakrisin*—Distinguishing, passing sentence on (Rom. 14:1); hence the ability to differentiate as to good and evil, to distinguish right and wrong.

CHAPTER 6

1   Therefore leaving behind the elementary teaching[1] about the Christ, let us be borne on to spiritual maturity, not laying again a foundation[2] of repentance from dead works, and of faith upon God,
2   of teaching about baptisms,[3] and of laying on of hands,[4] and of resurrection of the dead, and of eternal judgment.[5]
3   And this we will do, if God permit.[6]
4   For with reference to those once for all enlightened,[7] having both

---

1. *tēs archēs*—From *archē*, beginning, as of a book or of the gospel (Mark 1:1), origin, the first cause, hence, elementary teaching about the Christ.
2. *themelion*—From *themelios*, foundation stone, used also "of the elementary beginnings of a thing" (Bauer). Once the foundation stone for repentance and faith has been laid, it is laid, and not to be laid again.
3. *baptismōn*—Not necessarily a specific reference to Christian baptism but may refer to immersions or ablutions such as the mystery religions practiced and the Jews required of converts or proselytes.
4. *epitheseōs te cheirōn*—Laying on of hands. Common usage in New Testament times as "a sign of blessing" (Matt. 19:13), and of healing (Mark 7:32). See also Acts 6:6, Acts 8:17 ff., Acts 13:3, and 1 Timothy 4:14.
5. *krimatos aiōniou*—Eternal judgment, judgment that is endless and timeless.
6. *epitrepēi*—From *epitrepō*, permit, allow, order, instruct.
7. *hapax phōtisthentas, geusamenous . . . metochous*—Enlightened, tasted, partakers. Genuine spiritual experiences such as a believer has in his quest for salvation.

41

tasted of the heavenly gift and been made sharers of the Holy Spirit,
5   and having tasted the good word of God and the powers of the age
to come,

6   and having fallen away,[8] it is impossible to keep on restoring[9] *them*
unto repentance,[10] seeing they crucify to themselves the Son of God
and hold *Him* up to contempt.[11]

7   For land which has drunk the rain which frequently comes upon it and
produces usable vegetation[12] for those on whose account it is
cultivated, keep on receiving a blessing from God;

8   but land producing thorn plants and thistles *is* rejected[13] and near a
curse whose end is for burning.

9   But we are persuaded[14] concerning you, beloved, of better things,
that is things holding on to[15] salvation, even though we thus speak,

10   for God is not unjust as to forget[16] your work and the love which you

---

8.   *parapesontas*—From *parapiptō*, a verb to fall aside or along side, go
astray, miss something—a mark or a goal.

9.   *anakainizein*—From *anakainizō*, to restore, renew, make new.

10. *metanoian*—Change of mind, change "in the inner man" (Souter), remorse,
turning about, repentance, conversion.

11. *paradeigmatizontas*—From *paradeigmatizō*, put to open shame. Used
in a denigrating sense of making a public example of someone, for instance,
by punishment; to make an example of or expose. Hence, contempt.

12. *botanēn eutheton*—Herb, plant, fodder, weeds, and with *eutheton*, as
here, "vegetation suitable for food" (Polhill).

13. *adokimos*—Unapproved, counterfeit, "failing to pass the test" (Souter),
base, unqualified, hence, rejected.

14. *pepeismetha*—Perfect passive indicative of *peithō*, convince, persuade,
hence, stand persuaded.

15. *echomena*—From *echō*, have, hold, possess, used also in the sense of
preserve, keep, and of states of being: hold in one's grip, hold. Hence, holding
onto.

16. *epilathesthai*—From *epilanthanomai*—forget, care nothing about, neglect, overlook.

showed in His name, *in that you* ministered and continue to minister to the saints.

11 And we keep on longing for each one of you to show the same zeal[17] unto the fullness of the hope up to the end,

12 that you become not sluggish[18] but imitators of those who, through faith and patient endurance, inherit the promises.

X. God's Promise to Abraham (6:13-20)

13 For when God made promise[19] to Abraham, since He had no one greater to swear by, swore by Himself,

14 saying, Surely blessing I will bless[20] thee, and multiplying I will multiply thee;

15 and thus, having patiently endured,[21] he *(Abraham)* obtained the promise.

16 For men swear by the greater; and in their every dispute the oath is final for confirmation;[22]

17 wherein God, desiring to show more abundantly unto the heirs of the promise the unchangeable[23] character of His purpose, mediated with an oath,

18 that through two unchangeable things, in which it is impossible for God to lie, we who have fled for refuge may keep on having strong

---

17. *spoudēn*—From *spoudē*, speed, haste, anxiety, care, earnestness, eagerness, zeal.

18. *nōthroi*—Sluggish, lazy.

19. *epaggeilamenos*—From *epaggellō*, proclaim, announce, offer, or promise something to someone. Used of God's promises to His people.

20. *eulogēsō*—I will bless thee. See Genesis 22:16 ff.

21. *makrothumēsas*—From *makrothumeō*, wait, have patience, be patient, forbearing (first aorist active participle). A compound word from *makros*, *thumos*, meaning long spirit.

22. *eis bebaiōsin*—From *bebaiōsis*, gratification, establishment, confirmation.

23. *ametatheton*—From *ametathetos*, unchangeable.

encouragement[24] to hold fast to the hope that is set before us:

19 which we have as an anchor[25] of the soul, both firm and secure, and entering the inner *sanctuary* of the curtain[26] *(the holy of holies),*

20 where Jesus, going before us,[27] entered in our behalf having become High Priest forever according to the order of Melchizedek.

---

24. *paraklēsin*—From *paraklēsis*, encouragement, exhortation, appeal, request, also consolation, comfort.
25. *agkuran*—From *agkura*, anchor, as the anchor of a ship.
26. *esōteron*—From *esōteros*, inner, as the inner part of a prison (Acts 16:24). The space inside the curtain—the Holy of Holies.
27. *prodromos*—Of one who goes before or in advance to a place where someone else is to follow. Forerunner as of a scout sent ahead to make observations.

CHAPTER 7

XI. Jesus and the Priestly Order—the Old and the New (7:1-28)

1   For this Melchizedek,[1] king of Salem, priest of the Most High God,
    who met Abraham returning from the slaughter of the kings[2] and
    blessed him,

2   and to whom Abraham apportioned a tithe[3] of everything, being
    first, by interpretation, king of righteousness and then also king of
    Salem, which is king of peace,

3   without father, without mother, without genealogy, having neither
    beginning of days nor end of life, but made like unto the Son of God,
    he remains a priest forever.[4]

---

1. *Melchisedek*—The same Melchizedek previously mentioned, and whose
   priesthood is older and of a higher order than that of Aaron. See Genesis
   14:18-20 and Psalm 110. As king and priest of Salem he was without
   predecessor and without successor.
2. *basileōn*—Kings: Amraphel, Arioch, Chedorlaomer, Tidal.
3. *dekatēn*—A tenth. Even the heathen conquerors gave a tenth of the spoils of
   war to their gods; but here Abraham gave tithes to Melchizedek as God's
   priest.
4. *eis to diēnekes*—Continuous, uninterrupted, forever. Here the comparison
   of Melchizedek with Christ is carried still further.

4   See how great[5] this man was to whom [also] Abraham the patriarch[6] gave a tithe out of the chief booty.

5   And they indeed of the sons of Levi that receive the priestly office have a commandment to collect a tithe[7] from the people (that is, from their brothers) according to the law, although they have descended from Abraham;

6   but the one whose ancestry is not traced from them received tithes from Abraham, and blessed him that has the promises.[8]

7   And beyond all dispute[9] the inferior is blessed by the superior.

8   And here[10] on the one hand dying men receive the tithes, but there one of whom it is witnessed that he lives.[11]

9   And so to speak, through Abraham[12] Levi also who receives tithes has paid tithes,

10   for he was still in the loins of his forefather[13] when Melchizedek met him.

---

5. *pēlikos*—How great, how large, here in the sense of distinctiveness, "how distinguished" (Robertson).

6. *patriarchēs*—From *patria*, tribe, and *archō*, to rule. Hence, the word *patriarch*. Abraham was patriarch (father) of the Hebrew nation.

7. *apodekatoun*—From *apodekatoō*, "In active, collect a tithe. In passive, pay a tithe" (Polhill).

8. *epaggelias*—The promises. Note the frequent allusion to God's promises to Abraham (Gen. 12:3,7; 13:14; 17:5; 22:16-18).

9. *antilogias*—Contradiction, dispute. Here the idea is that the matter is beyond "all doubt."

10. *kai hōde*—And here, that is, with reference to the Levitical system, while "there" has reference to Melchizedek.

11. *zēi*—(present indicative, and hence the continuous idea) He lives. That is, there is nothing in the Genesis record to indicate the contrary.

12. *di' Abraam*—Through Abraham, the representative of the Jewish people. Hence, all his descendants are included in him not only physically but in relation to the promises of God.

13. *tou patros*—His father, that is, Abraham, who was the ancestor of Levi.

11   Now if indeed there were perfection[14] through the Levitical priesthood (for on the basis of it the people had received the law), what further need was there for another priest to arise according to the order of Melchizedek and not be reckoned according to the order of Aaron?

12   For the priesthood being changed, there becomes of necessity[15] also a change of the law.

13   For He[16] of whom these things are spoken belonged to a different tribe from which no one has officiated at the altar;

14   for it is evident[17] to all that our Lord has sprung out of Judah, with reference to which tribe Moses said nothing about priests,

15   and it is still more abundantly clear,[18] if according to the likeness of Melchizedek there arises another priest,

16   who has been made not according to the law of a carnal commandment,[19] but according to the power of an indissoluble life,[20]

---

14. *teleiōsis*—Perfection, that is fulfillment, a bringing to completion the purposes of God through the Levitical priesthood. In other words, if everything were all right as it was, with reference to the priesthood, why the order of Melchizedek? Why not let the order of Aaron continue?

15. *ex anagkēs*—Compulsion, necessity "of any kind, outer or inner, brought about by the nature of things, a divine dispensation, some hoped-for advantage, custom, duty" (Bauer).

16. *hon*—That is, "Our Lord" (v. 14).

17. *prodēlon*—From *prodēlos*, an old adjective meaning clear, known to all, evident, also used in the sense of reveal, make clear. The relationship of Jesus to the tribe of Judah was clear to all.

18. *perissoteron eti katadēlon*—More abundantly evident, clearer still. The record is there, and it should be evident to all.

19. *entolēs sarkinēs*—Carnal commandment, that is, the Levitical priest received the office by birth.

20. *zōēs akatalutou*—Endless life. Life that is indissoluble, that cannot be broken up (Souter).

17   for it is witnessed[21] of *Him*

> "Thou art a priest forever
> according to the order of Melchizedek."

18   For indeed on the one hand there takes place the annulment[22] of a preceding commandment because of its weakness and uselessness

19   (for the law made nothing perfect), and a bringing in besides of a better hope[23] through which we come near to God.

20   And inasmuch as *it is* not without the taking of an oath

21   (for they[24] indeed have been made priests without an oath but He[25] with an oath; by the One speaking with reference to Him

> The Lord swore with an oath
> and He will not change His mind,
> Thou *art* a priest forever);

22   by so much [also] Jesus has become the guarantee[26] of a better covenant.

23   And they who have been made priests are indeed many in number because of being prevented[27] by death from continuing;

24   but He, because He abides forever, holds the priesthood permanently.[28]

---

21. *martureitai*—From *martureō*, I bear witness, I give evidence, I testify; in the passive voice, I am witnessed to, I am borne witness to.

22. *athetēsis*—Annulment in a legal sense, also the general idea of removal.

23. *kreittonos elpidos*—Better hope, for through it all men may "draw nigh unto God."

24. *hoi*—They of the Levitical order.

25. *ho de*—But He, meaning Jesus, the Messiah, was qualified by the Lord who appointed Him a priest forever.

26. *egguos*—Security, a surety, an old adjective "under good security," and guarantee when used as a noun. Hence, "a guarantee of the better covenant."

27. *dia . . . kōluesthai*—"Because of them being hindered" (Robertson), the Levitical priest had to die like everyone else, but not so of Jesus.

28. *eis ton aiōna*—Permanently, unending.

25   Therefore He is able also to save[29] for all time those coming through Him to God, always living to make intercession for them.

26   For such a High Priest was also fitting[30] for us, holy, guileless, undefiled, separated from the sinners, and having become higher than the heavens;

27   who has not daily need,[31] just as the high priests did first in behalf of their own sins to offer up sacrifices, and then for the sins of the people; for this He did, once for all,[32] when He offered up Himself.

28   For the law[33] appoints men high priests having weakness; but the word of the oath, which was after the law, *appoints* a Son made perfect forever.

---

29. *sōzein eis to panteles dunatai*—Able to save, that is to rescue, to preserve, to deliver—and that "for all time" those who come through Him to God.

30. *eprepen*—Imperfective active indicative of *prepō*, suit, hence, fitting. Fitting because in His character Jesus, our great High Priest, was like unto Melchizedek, "and made higher than the heavens."

31. *ouk echei . . . anagkēn*—Jesus has no need whether daily or any other time to do as the high priests formerly did in their offering of sacrifices in behalf of their own sins as well as for the sins of the people.

32. *ephapax*—"Once for all." What a contrast between Jesus, and the Levitical priests!

33. *ho nomos . . . ho logos*—"The law . . . the word." What the law could not do, The word of the oath taking after the law did through the appointment of Jesus, God's Son, as a perfect High Priest forever.

CHAPTER 8

XII. Jesus and the New Covenant (8:1-13)

1 Now the main point[1] in what we are saying *is this:* We have such a
   High Priest,[2] who sat down at the right hand of the throne of the
   Majesty in the heavens,

2 a Minister of the holy places and of the real Tent (tabernacle),[3] which
   the Lord set up, not man,

3 for every high priest is appointed for the offering of both gifts and
   sacrifices; hence it is necessary[4] that this One also have somthing that
   He may offer.

4 If indeed therefore He were on earth,[5] not at all would He be a

---

1. *kephalaion* (from *kephalē,* head)—Hence, main thing or point, the heart
   of the matter, "the pith."

2. *toiouton . . . archierea*—Such a High Priest. In the verses that follow the
   writer outlines in detail the superiority of Jesus as High Priest.

3. *tēs skēnēs tēs alēthinēs*—The earthly tabernacle in which Aaron served
   was but a symbol of the heavenly tabernacle. Hence, "the real tabernacle" or
   "genuine tabernacle," pitched by the Lord and not by man.

4. *anagkaion*—It is necessary, that is "a moral and logical necessity"
   (Robertson). See Acts 13:46; Philippians 1:24.

5. *epi gēs*—On earth, in contrast to His role as a priest in heaven. After all,
   those looking to the law for salvation have their earthly priest to offer gifts in
   their behalf.

priest, since there are those offering the gifts according to the law,
5   who serve a model and shadow[6] of the heavenly things just as Moses
was given a revelation of God when he (Moses) was about to
complete the tent; for, "See," He says, "that you make everything
according to the pattern that was shown you on the mountain."
6   But now He (Christ) has attained[7] a more excellent ministry,[8] by so
much as He is also mediator of a better covenant[9] which has been
enacted upon better promises.[10]
7   For if that first covenant[11] were faultless, there would have been no
place[12] sought for a second.
8   For, finding fault[13] with them He says,
        Behold, the days come, says the Lord,
        When I will make a new covenant[14] with the house of Israel
            and with the house of Judah;

---

6. **hupodeigmati kai skiai**—A copy and shadow of the heavenly things. "A
    shadowy outline" (Moffatt).
7. **tetuchen**—Perfect active indicative of **tugchano,** to attain, to hit the mark,
    obtain.
8. **diaphorōteras . . . leitourgias**—A more excellent ministry. Note how this
    qualifying expression marks all five points of the superiority of Jesus'
    priesthood over the Levitical.
9. **kreittonos diathēkēs**—A better covenant, better than the promises God
    made to Abraham in the old covenant.
10. **kreittosin epaggeliais**—Better promises. Any way the comparison turns,
    the priesthood of Christ is superior.
11. **he prōtē ekeinē (diathēkēs)**—Actually the word covenant *(diathēkēs)*
    does not appear in the ancient manuscript, but the adjective first *(prōtē)* is
    feminine and implies the word covenant.
12. **ouk . . . topos**—Place, region, position, opportunity, possibility, chance.
13. **memphomenos**—From **memphomai,** blame, find fault with, as of one
    person with another.
14. **diathēkēn kainēn**—A new covenant—new in contrast to the old, new in the
    sense of unused, unknown, remarkable, along fresh lines.

9   Not according to the covenant that I made with their fathers
         On the day I took them by their hand[15] to lead them out of the
             land of Egypt
         For they remained not in My covenant,
         And I disregarded[16] them, says the Lord.

10   For this is the covenant that I will covenant with the house of
             Israel
         After those days, saith the Lord:
         Putting My laws into their mind,[17]
         And upon their hearts[18] I will write them,
         And I will be to them a God,
         And they shall be to Me a people.

11   And they shall not teach every one his fellow citizen,
         And every one his brother, saying, Know the Lord;
         For all[19] shall know Me[20] from the small to the great of them.

12   For I will be merciful[21] *in relation* to their iniquities,
         And their sins, I will remember no more.[22]

---

15.   *mou tēs cheiros*—A moving picture filled with tenderness and pathos.
16.   *ēmelēsa*—From *ameleō,* to neglect, be careless of, be unconcerned about someone or something, to disregard, pay no attention to.
17.   *eis tēn dianoian*—Mind, understanding, intelligence.
18.   *epi kardias autōn*—The heart was regarded as the core of a person's being, that with the mind rounded up everything significant in a human being.
19.   *esontai moi*—In the new covenant, all doubts are removed; the realization of the ideal set forth in the old covenant is now to be fully realized.
20.   *pantes eidēsousin me*—For all shall know me, yea, "from the small to the great of them." In the new covenant no one is to be left out, for it is to embrace every person of every race and every nation—as many as will enter into the covenant relationship by faith.
21.   *hileōs*—Merciful, gracious, forgiving, used repeatedly in the Bible to mark God's loving concern for people.
22.   *ou . . . eti*—Not yet, not still, not further, no more.

13   In the saying "new" *(covenant),* He has treated the first *covenant* as
          obsolete;[23] and that which is becoming obsolete and growing old is
          near disappearance.[24]

---

23. *palaioumenon*—Make old, "declare or treat as obsolete" (Bauer), in
     passive, become old in the sense of useless or obsolete.
24. *aphanismou*—From *aphanismos,* disappearance, destruction (Bauer).

CHAPTER 9

XIII. The Two Sanctuaries (9:1-22)

1   Now even the first covenant used to have regulations[1] for worship and the earthly sanctuary.

2   For a tent *(tabernacle)* was prepared, the first,[2] wherein were the lampstand and the table and the loaves of presentation,[3] which is called holy place;

3   and after the second curtain[4] a tent *(tabernacle)* which is called the holy of holies,

4   having a golden altar of incense, and the ark of the covenant[5] covered on all sides with gold in which *was* a golden jar holding the

---

1. *dikaiōmata*—Requirement, regulation, commandment. Used also in the sense of righteous deed.

2. *hē prōtē*—There were two divisions in the larger tent (the first and the second). The first place of entry was called *hagia* (holy). This was the first division of the tabernacle.

3. *hē prothesis tōn artōn*—Loaves of presentation, that is, the loaves of God's presence.

4. *deuteron . . . skēnē*—Second curtain, the curtains separating the first tabernacle from the second.

5. *kibōton tēs diathēkēs*—Ark of the covenant. A chest or box two- and one-half cubits long, one-and-a-half cubits in breadth, and a cubit-and-a-half in height. See Exodus 25:10 ff.

manna and the rod of Aaron that sprouted, and the stone tablets of the covenant;

5 and above it cherubim[6] of glory overshadowing the mercy seat;[7] concerning which things we cannot now speak in detail.

6 Now these things having been thus prepared, the priests go into the first tabernacle continually,[8] performing the rituals,

7 but into the second tabernacle, the high priest alone[9] once a year, not without blood, which he offers for himself, and for the sins of the people committed in ignorance;[10]

8 the Holy Spirit making this clear that the way into the holy place has not yet been made manifest,[11] while the first tabernacle is still standing,

9 which is a figure[12] for the present time, according to which are offered both gifts and sacrifices that are unable[13] in relation to the conscience to make perfect the one worshiping,

---

6. *cheroubin*—From *cheroub*, cherub, two-winged figure whose shadow fell on the mercy seat.

7. *to hilastērion*—The mercy seat, "that which expiates or propitiates" (Bauer). The mercy seat was not in itself the propitiatory gift, but rather represented the place of propitiation.

8. *dia pantos eisiasin*—Priests went in continually to perform their rituals—an unceasing performance.

9. *monos ho archiereus*—Alone, and only once each year the high priest entered the second tabernacle taking with him a blood offering for himself and for the sins of the people.

10. *agnoēmatōn*—Sins of ignorance, that is, sins committed in ignorance by the people.

11. *mēpō pephanerōsthai*—From *phaneroō*, to make plain. The first "way" into the holy place was merely a shadow typifying the way that was yet to come.

12. *parabolē*—Literally, comparison, hence, figure, type, illustration, parable.

13. *mē dunamenai*—Not able, that is, in the "age of crisis" (the present time) to satisfy the conscience. These gifts and sacrifices were not enough; they were only a type of the true sacrifice yet to come.

10 *dealing* only in the matter of meats and drinks and different washings,[14] regulations for the body, imposed until the time of the new order.

11 But Christ having come, a High Priest of good things realized already[15] through the greater and more perfect tabernacle, not made with hands—that is, not of this creation—

12 and not through the blood of goats and calves, but through His own blood,[16] He entered once for all[17] into the holy place, having obtained eternal redemption.

13 For if the blood of goats and bulls and ashes of a heifer sprinkling them who are ceremonially unclean, sanctify[18] unto ritualistic purity of the flesh,

14 by how much more shall the blood of Christ, who through the eternal Spirit offered Himself without blemish[19] to God, cleanse[20] our conscience from dead works to serve the living God?

---

14. *diaphorois baptismois*—Different washings, a reference to the ceremonial immersions of the Jews.

15. *tōn genomenōn agathōn*—Good things realized already, for Christ is now on the scene, and everything is changed.

16. *dia de tou idiou haimatos*—Through His own blood rather than through the blood of "goats and calves," which were only a figure, a shadow of His own sacrifice.

17. *ephapax*—At one time, at once, once for all. The arresting contrast between the high priesthood of Jesus and that of others who had gone before Him.

18. *hagiazei*—From *hagiazō*, dedicate, consecrate, sanctify, regard as holy, purify, to set things aside or make them acceptable for ritual purposes.

19. *amōmon*—From *amōmos*, a word used of sacrificial animals that are free from blemishes, or defects, hence blameless. Pilate could find no fault with Jesus, and Peter said He did "no sin."

20. *kathariei*—From *katharizō*, purify, cleanse from the defilement of sins, make one clean. Found by Deissmann in the inscriptions for ceremonial cleansing.

15 And because of this He is the mediator[21] of a new covenant, so that a death having taken place for redemption from the transgressions against the first covenant, they that have been called may receive the promise of the eternal inheritance.[22]

16 For where there is a last will and testament, the death of him who made it must be[23] made publicly known,

17 for the will is valid in the case of dead people, since it is never operative[24] while the one who made it is living.

18 Hence not even the first *covenant* has been inaugurated without blood.[25]

19 For when every commandment, according to the law, had been spoken by Moses to all the people, having taken the blood of the calves [and of the goats], with water and red wool and hyssop,[26] he sprinkled both the book itself[27] and all the people,

---

21. *mesitēs*—An arbitrator, mediator, here the go-between with humanity and God, an intermediary.

22. *aiōniou klēronomias*—Eternal inheritance. Herein lies the purpose of the incarnation, and this is why the mediatorial work of Christ surpasses that of other priests. His work is done once for all and brings to the faithful person an eternal inheritance.

23. *anagkē*—Here again the old word that implies compulsion, necessity; in this case the death of the person who made the will is necessary if the will is to be implemented.

24. *mēpote ischuei*—From *ischuō*, be powerful, strong, competent, be valid, have meaning.

25. *chōris haimatos*—In the first covenant after the burnt offerings and the peace offerings, the blood was sprinkled upon the altar and over the people, half and half. In the new covenant, only the blood of Christ was shed.

26. *hussōpou*—From *hussōpos*, "a small bush with blue flowers and highly aromatic leaves; used in purificatory sacrifices" (Bauer). See Exodus 12:22; Leviticus 14:4; Numbers 19:6,18.

27. *to Biblion*—The book of which no mention is made in the Exodus account of the sprinkling of the blood of the covenant.

20 saying, This is "the blood of the covenant[28] which God commanded to you";

21 and the tent *(tabernacle)* and also the vessels used in priestly service he sprinkled[29] likewise with the blood.

22 And almost everything is cleansed with blood, according to the law, and apart from the pouring out of blood[30] there is no forgiveness of *sin*.

XIV. Christ's Superior Sacrifice (9:23 to 10:18)

23 *It was* necessary therefore for the copies[31] of the things in the heavens to be cleansed with these; but the heavenly things themselves with better sacrifices[32] than these.

24 For Christ entered not into a holy place made with hands,[33] a copy of the true, but into heaven itself, now to appear before the face of God in our behalf;[34]

25 and not that He might offer Himself frequently[35] even as the high priest enters into the holy place annually with blood not his own;

---

28. *diathēkēs*—The covenant, that is, the first covenant, the old covenant.

29. *erantisen*—From *rantizō,* sprinkle, purify, used of the right of purification (Num. 19). Hence, cleanse, purify—a person or thing.

30. *haimatekchusias*—The pouring out or shedding of blood, a ceremonial act of cleansing according to the law of the old covenant. Otherwise there would be no forgiveness of sin.

31. *hupodeigmata*—Pattern, example, model, imitation, copy, hence, copies of the things in the heavens.

32. *kreittosin thusiais*—Better sacrifices. Another mark of the superiority of the priesthood of Jesus. He offered a better sacrifice.

33. *cheiropoiēta*—From *cheiropoiētos,* used of buildings or temples built by human hands.

34. *huper hēmōn*—Herein lies the heart of Christ's suffering on the cross: it was in our behalf—in behalf of all people.

35. *oud' . . . pollakis*—Not . . . frequently. The high priest entered into the holy place continually and with the blood "belonging to another" but not so of Christ. He entered "once for all" and with His own blood.

26   otherwise it would have been necessary for Him to suffer often, from
      the foundation of the world; but now once for all[36] at the end of the
      ages He has been manifested for the removal of [the] sin through the
      sacrifice of Himself.[37]

27   And just as it is laid up for men once to die,[38] and after this the
      judgment,[39]

28   so also the Christ, having been offered once to bear the sins of many,
      shall appear a second time,[40] without relation to sin, to them that
      eagerly await Him unto salvation.[41]

---

36.   *nuni de hapax*—Once for all. Christ's entrance into the holy place was
      once, and that one instance was final.

37.   *dia tēs thusias autou*—Through the sacrifice of Himself. He was the
      intermediary, the intermediate agent that continues to accomplish forgiveness
      for all of every race and nation who look to Him by faith for forgiveness and
      transformation.

38.   *hapax apothanein*—Once to die. No place in this premise for reincarna-
      tion on the earth, as some would have it.

39.   *krisis*—*Judgment,* judging, condemnation, and even punishment, when the
      judgment relates to a person. From this word comes our English word *crisis.*
      And here is the real crisis that humanity without exception will face at the last
      day—the crisis of the judgment of God.

40.   *ek deuterou*—From *deuteros,* "purely numerical" (Bauer). Used with
      reference to a series, or place like the second sentinel's post (Acts 12:10) or the
      second curtain (Heb. 9:3). A clear reference to the Second Coming of Christ,
      and this time without reference to sin.

41.   *sōtērian*—Salvation, the final aspect of total deliverance (salvation) to be
      realized by all who "eagerly await Him."

CHAPTER 10

1   For the law having a shadow of the good things to come, not the very image[1] of the things, can never with the same sacrifices which they offer continually year by year make perfect those coming to God.

2   Otherwise, would they not have ceased[2] to be offered because those worshiping, having been cleansed once for all, would have had no more consciousness of sins?

3   But in those *sacrifices there is* a reminder[3] of sins each year,

4   for it is impossible[4] for the blood of bulls and goats to take away sins.

5   Therefore coming[5] into the world He says,
      Sacrifice and offering Thou hast not desired
      But a body Thou didst prepare[6] for Me;

6   With regard to whole burnt offerings and *sacrifices* for sin Thou hast taken no delight.[7]

---

1. *ouk autēn tēn eikona*—The very image, likeness, form, appearance—note the difference between a shadow *(skian)* and "the very image."
2. *epausanto*—From *pauō*, cause to stop, stop, cease.
3. *anamnēsis*—Remembrance of something, reminder, call to mind.
4. *adunaton*—From *adunatos*, impotent, powerless, impossible—a flat impossibility.
5. *eiserchomenos*—A reference to Christ's incarnation.
6. *katērtisō*—From *katartizō*, to equip, make ready.
7. *eudokēsas*—From *eudokeō*, consent, consider good, be well pleased, take delight, delight in, like, approve.

7   Then said I, Lo, I have come (in the roll of the book it is written[8] of Me),
       To do, O God, Thy will,

8   saying above[9] that Sacrifices and offerings and whole burnt offerings, and *sacrifices* for sins Thou didst neither desire nor find pleasure *therein* (which are offered according to the law).

9   Then He said, "Lo, I am come to do Thy will." He abolishes[10] the first that He may establish the second.

10 By which will we have been sanctified[11] through the offering of the body of Jesus Christ once for all.

11 And indeed every priest stands daily[12] ministering and offering frequently the same sacrifices, which can never[13] take away sins,

12 but He (Christ), when He had offered one sacrifice[14] for sins forever, sat down at the right hand of God,

13 from now on waiting expectantly[15] until His enemies be made a footstool of His feet;

14 for by one offering He has perfected forever[16] those being sanctified.

---

8. *gegraptai*—Perfect passive indicative from *graphō,* write. It has been written, it stands written.

9. *anōteron*—From *anōteros,* meaning higher; also above, or earlier, in referring to a previous statement. Christ is speaking as in verse 5.

10. *anairei*—From *anaireō,* do away with, take away, destroy.

11. *hēgiasmenoi*—Set apart by or for God, hence, holy, sacred, sanctified.

12. *kath' hēmeran*—Day by day. An endless ritual, and yet to no lasting avail.

13. *oudepote*—Never, that is, not at any time. The priestly offerings had no power to take away sins.

14. *mian ... thusian*—One sacrifice, and one only, and that is never repeated. Here the contrast is sharp and clear between the Levitical priest and Christ as the great High Priest.

15. *ekdechomenos*—From *ekdechomai,* to wait (for someone), expect, hence, wait expectantly (see 1:13).

16. *teteiōken eis to diēnekes*—Perfect tense here. Christ by one offering accomplished what the Levitical priest could never do. And the accomplishment is still holding, still "going on."

15 And the Holy Spirit also bears witness[17] to us; for after having said,
16   This is the covenant that I will covenant with them
   After those days, saith the Lord;
   Having put My laws upon their heart,[18]
   I will also write them upon their mind;
17   And their sins and their transgressions I will remember no
   more.[19]
18 Now where *there is* forgiveness of these *there is* no more offering[20]
for sin.

XV. Encouragement to Steadfastness in Faith (10:19-39)

19 Having therefore, brothers, boldness for the entrance into the holy
place by the blood of Jesus,[21]
20 which way He opened[22] for us, a new and living way through the
curtain, that is, His flesh;
21 and *having* a great priest[23] at the house of God,
22 let us keep on coming *to God* with a true heart in full assurance[24] of

---

17. *marturei*—From *martureo*, be a witness, bear witness, bear witness to,
confirm, declare, testify favorably.
18. *kardias . . . dianoian*—Hearts and mind. This verse harks back to 8:10 with
some changes, but with no alteration of the meaning.
19. *ou mē . . . eti*—No longer, no more. The former sins are forgiven forever.
20. *ouketi prosphora*—No further offering for sins. The matter of repetitive
sacrifices is needless and uncalled for, now that Christ has made the supreme
offering for sins.
21. *haimati 'Iēsou*—Now the holy place is entered, not by the blood of animals,
but by the precious blood of Jesus who, as Lamb of God, "taketh away the sin
of the world!" (John 1:29).
22. *enekainisen*—From *egkanizō*, open a way, renew, do anew, to initiate,
dedicate, consecrate. And the new way is a living *(zōsan)* way.
23. *hierea megan*—Great High Priest. As has been clearly revealed in 4:14 to
7:28.
24. *plērophoriai*—Certainty, full assurance, full conviction.

faith, having had our hearts sprinkled[25] from an evil conscience, and having had our body washed with pure water.

23   Let us keep on holding fast the confession of our hope without wavering,[26] for faithful *is* He that promised;

24   and let us keep on considering one another unto the stirring up[27] of love and good works,

25   not forsaking[28] our own assembling together as the habit[29] is with some people, but encouraging *one another* and by so much the more as you see the Day drawing near.[30]

26   For when we are deliberately[31] sinning after having received the knowledge of the truth, there no longer[32] remains a sacrifice for sins,

27   but a certain fearful expectation[33] of judgment, and intense heat of fire that is about to devour the adversaries.

28   Whoever has set at naught the law of Moses dies without mercy[34] on

---

25. *hrerantismenoi . . . lelousmenoi*—Sprinkled . . . washed, expressions harking back to the ancient "outward sacramental signs of cleansing" (Westcott).

26. *aklinē*—From *aklinēs*, without wavering, inclining away from the confession.

27. *paroxusmon*—From *paroxusmos*, spurring, encouragement in behalf of love and good works. The word is also used in the sense of provoking that results in irritation or wrath.

28. *mē egkataleipontes*—From *egkataleipō*, forsake, abandon, desert, leave behind, leave.

29. *ethos*—Usage, custom, habit, as of the customs of a country, or of one's family habits.

30. *eggizousan*—From *eggizō*, come near, approach. The reference here is to the approaching day of the final realization of salvation. There is no timetable for such, but certainly every passing day brings the grand event nearer.

31. *hekousiōs*—Willingly, intentionally, deliberately.

32. *ouketi*—No longer, no more, no further.

33. *ekdochē*—All that remains in such a situation is "fearful expectation of judgment."

34. *chōris oiktirmōn*—From *oiktirmos*, pity, compassion, mercy.

the testimony of two or three witnesses;

29   by how much severer punishment[35] do you think he shall be counted worthy who has trampled under foot the Son of God, and has regarded unclean[36] the blood of the covenant with which He was sanctified, and has insulted the Spirit of the grace?

30   For we know Him who said,

         Vengeance[37] is Mine, I will repay.

     And again,

         The Lord will judge[38] His people.

31   *It is fearful[39] to fall into the hands of the living God.*

32   But remember[40] the former days in which, having been enlightened, you continued to endure a hard struggle of sufferings,

33   sometimes being publicly exposed[41] both to reproaches and afflictions, and sometimes having become comrades of those living in such circumstances.

34   For you both sympathized with the prisoners and accepted[42] the

---

35. *timōrias*—Punishment, penalty, vengeance. Vengeance appears to be the older idea of the word *timōria*.

36. *koinon*—From *koinos*, old idea shared, common; in Hebraistic use, unclean, unwashed, dirty, profane, in contrast to *hagios*, holy.

37. *enubrisas*—From *enubrizō*, insult, outrage, by rudeness of speech or other action that is denigrating, defaming, by casting aspersions on.

38. *krinei*—From *krinō*, judge, decide, reach a decision, condemn, pass judgment on. God is the final arbiter, not man.

39. *phoberon*—From *phoberos*, something that causes fear, is fearful, frightful, terrible.

40. *anamimnēiskesthe*—From *anamimnēskō*, present middle imperative. Hear, hence, "remind yourselves," call to mind, remember.

41. *theatrizomenoi*—From *theatrizō*, expose publicly, put to shame, make a public show of, expose to public shame, "being made a gazing-stock" (Robertson).

42. *prosedexasthe*—From *prosdechomai*, welcome, receive, accept. They reacted joyfully to the plundering hands of the cruel invaders.

plundering of your belongings with joy, knowing that you yourselves have a better possession and one that is permanent.[43]

35 Cast not away therefore your confidence[44] which has a great reward.

36 For you have need of patient endurance,[45] that, having done the will of God, you may receive the promise.

37   For yet a very little while,
           He that is coming[46] shall come and shall not linger;

38   But My righteous one shall live by faith,
           And if he should draw back,[47]
           My soul has no pleasure in him.

39 But we[48] are not of *them* who retreat unto destruction, but of *them* who have faith unto the saving of the soul.

---

43. *menousan*—From *menō*, abide, remain, wait for, await. Their treasures were in heaven (Matt. 6:19 ff.).

44. *parrēsian*—Freedom, boldness, liberty, frankness, outspokenness, fearlessness, courage, confidence.

45. *hupomonēs*—Steadfastness, endurance, constancy, patient, steadfast, waiting for, "a patient enduring" (Thayer).

46. *ho erchomenos*—He that is coming, a messianic reference.

47. *huposteilētai*—From *hupostello,* in middle voice, as here, shrink from, draw back, avoid, also the idea of keeping silent is sometimes present.

48. *hēmeis*—But we, in stark contrast to those who beat a retreat "unto destruction."

CHAPTER 11

XVI. Faith and Its Works in the Lives of God's People (11:1-40)

1   Now faith is the title deed[1] of things hoped for, a conviction about things not seen.
2   For therein the elders[2] were testified to.
3   By faith we understand that the worlds have been created[3] by the word of God, so that what is seen has been made out of things which do not appear.[4]

---

1. *hupostasis*—Widely used and with different meanings in the ancient inscriptions. Reality, actual being, nature, essence, situation, condition, realization, assurance, confidence (literally an underlying—Souter), hence, foundation.
2. *presbuteroi*—From *presbutēs*, and aged man, old man, advanced in life, signifying rank or office among the Jews as of members of the Sanhedrin or great council; among Christians, the term was used of those who presided over the assemblies or churches (Thayer). A term used along with our word *pastor*, and *bishop*, to apply to early ministries of the gospel. The use here possibly may refer more, in a general sense, to "the fathers" rather than the technical sense of elders as commonly found in the New Testament.
3. *katērtisthai*—From *katartizō*, restore, put in order, complete, make complete, prepare, make, create.
4. *phainomenōn*—From *phainō*, act., to give light, shine, be bright; in middle or passive voice: flash, shine, be revealed, appear, become visible, make one's appearance, appear as something, have the appearance of, "to have the outward appearance of being something" (Bauer).

4   By faith Abel offered a more *acceptable* sacrifice[5] to God than Cain,
        through which he was witnessed to that he was righteous, God
        bearing witness to his gifts, and through it (his faith)[6] having died yet
        he keeps on speaking.

5   By faith Enoch was translated[7] so as not to see death; and he was still
        not found, because God took him up; for before the translation he
        had witness borne to him that he had been well pleasing to God.

6   And without faith it is impossible to be well pleasing *to Him*, for it is
        necessary for the one coming to God to believe that He exists[8] and
        that He becomes a rewarder[9] to those who search for Him.

7   By faith Noah being warned *of God* concerning things not yet seen,
        and being moved with reverent awe, constructed an ark for the
        deliverance[10] of his household, through which[11] he condemned the
        world, and became heir of the righteousness that is according to
        faith.

8   By faith Abraham, being called,[12] obeyed to go out unto a place

---

5. *pleiona thusian*—Literally, "more sacrifice" (comparative of adjective
    polus, much).

6. *di' autēs*—Through it, that is through Abel's faith which prompted "a better
    sacrifice."

7. *metethēkēn*—From *metatithēmi*, to change, to transpose, as in 7:12,
    literally to put in another place, convey to another place, alter, change, etc.
    Our word *metastasis* comes from this same Greek word.

8. *estin*—From the verb *eimi*, to be, exist, live.

9. *misthapodotēs*—A rewarder (Lit. "one who pays wages"), as of God
    (Bauer).

10. *eis sōtērian*—From *sōtēria*, used commonly for deliverance, preservation
    from impending danger. Our common word *salvation*. The idea of deliverance
    seems always to be present in the use of the word.

11. *di' hēs*—Through which, that is, through his faith, the faith manifested in the
    construction of an ark "for the deliverance of his household."

12. *kaloumenos*—From *kaleo*, called, as by name, provide with a name,
    address a person by name, designate. The Christian ministry is a divine
    calling.

which he was about to receive for an inheritance; and he went out not knowing[13] where he was going.

9   By faith he lived as a stranger[14] in the land of the promise, as in a *land* belonging to another, dwelling in tents with Isaac and Jacob, fellow heirs of the same promise;

10   for he kept on looking[15] for the city having the foundations[16] whose architect and builder *is* God.

11   By faith even Sarah herself, being barren and beyond the right time of age, received power for the sowing[17] of seed,[18] since she counted Him faithful who had promised;

12   wherefore also were born from one man, and that as good as dead,[19] *descendants* as the stars of heaven in number, and as the sand that is by the seashore, innumerable.

13   These all died according to faith, not having received the promises, but having seen and greeted them from afar, and having confessed that they were strangers and sojourners[20] upon the earth.

---

13. *mē epistamenos*—From *epistamai,* understand, be acquainted with, know. Abraham was in total ignorance concerning his destination. He obeyed to go out completely by faith.

14. *hōs allotrian*—From *allotrios,* lit. not one's own, belonging to another, as "another man's servant," or "other people's property," alien, unsuitable. Used in the sense of "strange people," hence aliens.

15. *exedecheto*—Imperfect middle of *ekdechomai,* wait for, await.

16. *tous themelious*—Lit. foundation stone, foundation of a building. Fig. "of the elementary beginnings of a thing . . . " (Bauer).

17. *katabolēn*—From *katabolē,* beginning, sowing of seed, lit. cast down, thrown down, as in laying a foundation; hence, foundation, beginning.

18. *spermatos*—Our word *sperm.*

19. *kai tauta nenekrōmenou*—From *nekroō,* a verb "to make dead, to treat as dead" (Rom. 4:19). Used here by hyperbole (Robertson).

20. *xenoi kai parepidēmoi*—Strangers and sojourners, or, as we might say, foreigners and pilgrims *(parepidēmoi),* a sojourner from another land (Robertson).

14   For those saying such things make it clear[21] that they are seeking
      after a homeland.

15   And if, indeed, they had continued to think[22] of that *country* from
      which they had gone out, they would have kept on having an
      opportunity to return;

16   but now they long for a better country, that is a heavenly one:
      Therefore God is not ashamed of them, to be called their God; for
      He has prepared[23] for them a city.

17   By faith Abraham, being put to the test,[24] offered up Isaac; yea, he
      that received the promises was offering[25] his only son,

18   regarding whom it was said, "In Isaac shall thy seed be named."[26]

19   Having reckoned that God is able to raise up even from the dead;
      whence He also, in a figurative sense,[27] did receive him back.

---

21.   *emphanizousin*—From *emphanizō*, make visible, reveal, explain, inform,
      make known, make clear.

22.   *emnēmoneuon*—From *mnēmoneuō*, keep in mind, remember, think of. In
      other words, they were not look back so much as forward. They had an
      opportunity to return had they wanted to do so.

23.   *hētoimasen*—From *hetoimazō*, prepare, keep or put in readiness; in other
      words, God had made provisions in advance for them, and everything was
      ready and waiting.

24.   *peirazomenos*—From *peirazō*, put to the test, make trial of. The faith of
      Abraham was on trial. The verb *peirazomenos* is present passive participle.
      This means the test was filled in process.

25.   *prospheren*—From *prospherō*, bring (to), as someone or something to
      someone. Offer, bring, present as of offerings or gifts. The verb is imperfect
      active indicative, and this means, again, Abraham was in the process of
      offering up his son. It was going on at the moment when God interrupted him.
      By intent, he had already accomplished the sacrifice of his son.

26.   *klēthēsetai*—From *kaleō* (future passive), name, call by name, provide with
      a name.

27.   *en parabolēi*—In a parable, comparison, illustration, parable; lit. "*a
      placing* of one thing *by the side* of another" (Thayer), juxtaposition as of ships
      placed side by side in battle.

20 By faith, Isaac blessed Jacob and Esau even concerning things to come.[28]

21 By faith Jacob, when dying, blessed each of the sons of Joseph, and worshiped, *leaning* upon the top of his staff.[29]

22 By faith Joseph, when coming to the end[30] *of his life,* made mention[31] of the Exodus of the sons of Israel, and gave orders concerning his bones.

23 By faith Moses, when he was born, was hid three months by his parents because they saw that the child was handsome[32] and they were not afraid of the edict of the king.

24 By faith Moses, when he was grown up,[33] refused to be called a son of Pharaoh's daughter,

25 rather having chosen[34] to suffer together with the people of God than to have the temporary[35] pleasure of sin.

26 Having considered the reproach of the Christ greater riches[36] than

---

28. *mellontōn*—From *mellō*, intend, I am about to, but in the absolute form as here in the present participle, something that is coming, future, and as of something that is about to be or come to pass.

29. *epi to akron tēs hrabdou autou*—This phrase appears to convey the idea that as the old man worshiped he was "leaning" on the top of his staff. There is actually no word for "leaning" but the quotation, taken from the Septuagint which in turn came from the Hebrew, seems to allow this meaning.

30. *teleutōn*—From teleō, end, accomplish, finish, complete.

31. *emnēmoneusen*—From *mnēmoneuō*, think of, keep in mind, remember, mention.

32. *asteion*—Well-formed, beautiful, possessing charm, bodily grace, well-pleasing, acceptable, handsome.

33. *megas genomenos*—Lit., "having become great." See Exodus 2:11.

34. *helomenos*—From *haireō*, used here in the second aorist middle and means "to take for oneself a position" (Robertson). Hence, rather having chosen.

35. *proskairon*—From *proskairos*, temporary, transitory, lasting only for a time, a little while.

36. *meizona plouton*—Greater wealth, greater riches.

the treasures of Egypt, for he kept on looking away[37] unto the reward.

27   By faith he left Egypt, not fearing the wrath[38] of the king; for, as seeing Him who is invisible, he endured.

28   By faith he kept the Passover and the pouring[39] of the blood, that the one destroying the firstborn should not touch them.

29   By faith they crossed the Red Sea as through dry land, of which, taking trial,[40] the Egyptians were drowned.

30   By faith the walls of Jericho fell down, having been encircled[41] for seven days.

31   By faith Rahab the harlot perished not with them that were disobedient, having received[42] as guests the spies with peace.

32   And what more shall I say?[43] For time will fail me telling about Gideon, Barak, Samson, Jephthah, David, and Samuel and the prophets,

33   who through faith conquered kingdoms, brought about righteousness, obtained promises, shut[44] the mouths of lions,

---

37.   *apeblepen*—Imperfect of *apoblepō*, "for he was looking away," literally kept on looking away unto the reward.

38.   *thumon*—From *thumos*, rage, anger, wrath, passion.

39.   *proschusin*—Sprinkling, spreading, pouring, as of the blood on the door posts (Ex. 12:22). From *proscheō*, to pour to or on. Only here in the New Testament.

40.   *peiran*—From *peira*, a trial, an attempt, "to have an experience of" (Souter).

41.   *kuklōthenta*—From *kukloō*, surround, encircle, usually in a hostile manner, circle around, go around, as here.

42.   *dexamenē*—From *dechomai*, receive, take, take in hand, approve, accept, welcome (as in receiving a guest).

43.   *legō*—Shall I say. Present active subjunctive (deliberative). The idiom is both oratorical and literary (Robertson).

44.   *ephraxan*—From *phrassō*, stop, shut, close, lock, bar, stop or close the mouth.

34   quenched[45] the power of fire, escaped mouths of the sword, were made strong from weakness, became powerful in war, turned to flight armies of enemies.

35   Women received their dead by a resurrection; and others were tortured, not accepting their deliverance,[46] that they might obtain a better resurrection;

36   and others received a trial of derisive tortures[47] and scourgings, and in addition, chains and prison.

37   They were stoned, they were sawn[48] in two, they died by murder of the sword; they went around[49] in sheep skins, in goat skins, being needy, afflicted, ill treated.

38   Of whom the world was not worthy, wandering[50] about in deserts, and mountains, and caves, and in the holes of the earth.

39   And these all, having had witness borne to them through their faith, received not the promise,[51]

40   God having provided something better[52] concerning us, that apart from us, they should not be made perfect.

---

45.   *esbesan*—From **sbennumi**, extinguish, put out something, stifle, suppress.

46.   *apolutrōsin*—From **apolutrōsis**, a word used for "*buying back* a slave or a captive, *making him free* by payment of a ransom" (Bauer). Lit. release, acquittal, redemption, also condition of release or being released.

47.   *empaigmōn*—From **empaigmos**, mocking, scorn, derisive torture such as martyrs experienced.

48.   *epristhēsan*—From **priō, prizō** (**prion**, a saw), to saw (into), as a type of execution.

49.   *periēlthon*—From **perierchomai**, go around, wander, go about.

50.   *planōmenoi*—To wander, to go astray.

51.   *tēn epaggelian*—The promise, that is, the messianic promise which they did not live long enough to see (11:13).

52.   *kreitton ti*—See 8:6 where Christ is presented as mediator of a better covenant resting on better promises. The better covenant is the covenant of grace made possible by Christ's atoning death on Calvary.

CHAPTER 12

XVII. The Disciplined Life (12:1-13)

1 Therefore we also, having lying around[1] us so great a throng of witnesses, having laid aside every weight and the easily ensnaring[2] sin, with patience let us keep on running the race that is set before us,

2 looking away to Jesus, the founder and perfecter of the faith, who in place of the joy[3] that was set before Him endured the cross, despising shame, and has sat down at the right hand of the throne of God.

3 For consider[4] Him that endured such hostility against Himself by the sinners, that you become not weary, giving out[5] in your souls.

4 You have not yet resisted[6] unto blood struggling against the sin;

5 and you have forgotten the exhortation, which is spoken to you as to sons,

---

1. *perikeimenon*—From *perikeimai*, lie around, or be placed around, as of a throng of people who are surrounding someone.

2. *euperistaton*—Easily encircling, easily surrounding, easily besetting.

3. *anti tēs prokeimenēs autōi charas*—In behalf of the joy that was set before Him. A difficult phrase since the word *anti* has such varied uses. But the sense here seems to be "in behalf of," "answering to," or "in exchange for."

4. *analogisasthe*—From *analogizomai*, to compare, reckon up, to weigh, consider.

5. *ekluomenoi*—From *ekluō*, give out, become weary or slack, lose heart.

6. *antikatestēte*—From *antikathistēmi*, resist, oppose, place against.

My son, regard not lightly[7] the discipline of the Lord,
nor lose heart when being punished by Him;

6   For whom the Lord loves He disciplines,[8]
and He chastises[9] every son whom He receives.

7   In discipline, you must continue to endure.[10] As with sons, God deals with you[11]; for what son *is there* whom the father does not discipline?

8   But if you are without discipline, whereof all have been made partakers, then you are illegitimate[12] children and not sons.

9   Furthermore, we used to have the fathers of our flesh as disciplinarians, and we continued to respect them; shall we not not much more rather be in subjection to the Father of our spirits,[13] and live?

10   For they indeed, for a few days, used to discipline *us* as it seemed best to them, but He for *our* benefit,[14] that we may share His holiness.

11   But all discipline, indeed for the time being, seems not to be joyous but grievous[15]; yet, later it yields peaceable fruit of righteousness to those trained by it.

---

7. *mē oligōrei*—From *oligōreō*, to make light of something, think lightly of it, regard lightly.

8. *paideuei*—From *paideuō*, train, instruct, educate, bring up, give guidance, correct, practice (discipline), discipline.

9. *mastigoi*—From *mastigoō*, lit. "of flogging as a punishment used by the synagogue" (Bauer). Compare Deuteronomy 25:2 ff. Fig.—chastise, punish. Used also in the general sense of torment, afflict, mistreat.

10. *hupomenete*—From *hupomenō*, remain while others do not, or others flee, hold out, abide under, stand one's ground and wait for.

11. *prospheretai*—From *prospherō*, to bear or bring (to), as a gift or something to someone. Used of the offering or presentation of gifts and offerings. Here in the sense of meet with or deal with.

12. *nothoi*—From *nothos*, baseborn, born out of wedlock, illegitimate.

13. *tōi patri tōn pneumatōn*—Father of our spirits, that is, God.

14. *epi to sumpheron*—From *sumpherō*, to be profitable, confer a benefit, be advantageous, help, profit, be an advantage.

15. *lupēs*—From *lupē*, sorrow, affliction, grief, something that produces pain of spirit or mind.

12   Wherefore, straighten up the drooping hands[16] and the weakened[17] knees,

13   and make straight paths for your feet, that the limbs of the lame be not dislocated[18] (injured), but rather be healed.

XVIII. The Believer and God's Grace (12:14-29)

14   Strive for[19] peace with everyone, and for holiness, without which no one will see the Lord,

15   taking care,[20] lest there be someone excluded from the grace of God; lest any root of bitterness springing up cause trouble, and through it many become defiled;[21]

16   lest *there be* any fornicator[22] or profane person as Esau, who in exchange for a single meal gave up his own birthright.

17   For you know also that afterwards, when desiring to inherit the blessing, he was rejected; for he found no place for a change of mind[23] *in his father* although with tears he sought it.

---

16. *pareimenas*—From *pariēmi*, neglect, let pass, omit, disregard; but here in the perfect passive participlar use, listless, weakened, slackened, weary, drooping.

17. *paralelumena*—From *paraluō*, undo, disable, weaken, "weakened knees," as here. Used also of the paralytic in Luke 5:24.

18. *ektrapēi*—From *ektrepō*, turn away, turn, twist, put out of joint, dislocate, turn, turn away, be turned aside.

19. *diōkete*—From *diōkō*, pursue, run after, press on, hasten, persecute. Fig., as here, strive for, pursue, aspire, seek after.

20. *episkopountes*—From *episkopeō*, see (to it), take care, look at, oversee, care for.

21. *mianthōsin*—From *miainō*, defile, stain, as of ceremonial impurity, or by vices and sin which lead to moral defilement.

22. *pornos*—Person who engages in sexual relations outside of marriage, here of a "male prostitute," sexual immorality.

23. *metanoias gar topon ouch heuren*—He found no place for a change of mind (in Isaac his father [understood]). Here is a passage often misunderstood. The point at issue is tribal advantage and responsibility, as it related to Esau and his father and brother. The idea has not to do with eternal salvation.

18 For you have not come to something that can be touched,[24] and *that* has been burning with fire, and to darkness and gloom and a storm,

19 and to a sound of a trumpet, and to a voice of words,[25] which those having heard begged for no further message to be spoken to them;

20 for they could not endure[26] the command given: "If even a beast should touch the mountain, it shall be stoned."

21 And, so frightful was the sight[27] *that* Moses said, "I am terrified and trembling,"

22 but you have come to mount Zion and to the city of the living God, the heavenly Jerusalem, and to myriads of angels in festal gathering,[28]

23 and to the assembly[29] of the firstborn who are enrolled in heaven, and to God the Judge of all, and to the spirits of righteous ones made perfect,

24 and to Jesus the mediator of a new[30] covenant, and to the blood of sprinkling that speaks better than *that* of Abel.

---

24. *psēlaphōmenōi*—From *psēlaphaō*, to touch, to handle. The situation is not like that of Mount Sinai, though the same moving manifestations of God are present, but in a different form, a different order.

25. *phonēi hrēmatōn*—Same sense of the palpable presence of God reflected in verse 18.

26. *ouk epheron*—Imperfect of old verb *pherō*, to bear, carry, bring, carry or bear a burden.

27. *phantazomenon*—From *phantazō*, appear, make visible, become visible, spectacle, sight, an unusual phenomena as of a theophany.

28. *panēgurei*—From *panēguris*, "a festal gathering of the whole people to celebrate public games or other solemnities" (Thayer), hence, a public festal assembly or festive gathering.

29. *ekklēsiai*—Church in the general sense "of all the redeemed," as in Matthew 16:18; and Colossians 1:18; Ephesians 5:24-32; and similar, in meaning, to the words "the kingdom of God."

30. *neas*—New, young, recently born, youthful, used of persons who have been "born again."

25   See that you reject not[31] the One speaking; for if those did not
          escape who rejected the One warning them on earth, much more *we*
          shall not escape in turning ourselves away from the One *warning*
          from heaven.

26   Whose voice then shook[32] the earth; but now He has promised,
          saying, "Yet once more I will cause to tremble (shake) not only the
          earth but also the heaven."

27   And this *phrase,* "yet once more," indicates[33] the removal of the
          things that are shaken (as of things that have been made), that the
          things which are not shaken may remain.

28   Wherefore, receiving a kingdom that cannot be shaken, let us keep
          on[34] holding on to grace whereby we may continue to serve God in
          an acceptable manner, with reverence and awe;

29   for our God also is a consuming fire.[35]

---

31.   *paraitēsamenoi*—From *paraiteomai,* decline, reject, refuse; used also in
      the sense of request, ask for, in the reflexive sense, excuse oneself. A word
      much varied in usage.

32.   *esaleusen*—From *saleuō,* cause to move to and fro, shake, waver, totter,
      etc.

33.   *dēloi*—From *dēloō,* to make clear, reveal, show something to someone,
      indicate.

34.   *echōmen*—Let us keep on, let us keep on getting grace, present volitive
      subjunctive (active) of *echō,* which could also be translated "let us keep on
      having gratitude," but better the former meaning.

35.   *katanaliskon*—From *katanaliskō,* used of fire that consumes, hence, "our
      God is a consuming fire."

CHAPTER 13

XIX. The Christian and Social and Religious Duties (13:1-19)

1   Brotherly love[1] is to remain.
2   Do not overlook hospitality,[2] for thereby some, without knowing it,[3] have entertained angels.
3   Keep on remembering the prisoners,[4] as bound with them; those being mistreated, as being yourselves also in the body.
4   Marriage *is to be* held in honor among all—and the marriage bed[5] *is to be* undefiled: for fornicators and adulterers[6] God will judge.
5   Your life-style[7] *is to be* free from the love of money,[8] being content

---

1. *philadelphia*—Love of brother, love of sister, brotherly love, used in literature of blood brothers, but here of brothers and sisters in the Christian faith.
2. *philoxenias*—Love for strangers, hospitality.
3. *elathon*—From *lanthanō*, escape notice, be hidden, escape someone's notice.
4. *desmiōn*—From *desmios*, a prisoner. Used of Christians as well as others in prison (Acts 16:25,27; 23:18).
5. *koitē*—Bed in general, but in particular the marriage bed. Used also as a euphemism for sexual intercourse.
6. *moichous*—From *moichos*, adulterer, one who has intercourse with another man's wife or vice versa whereas fornication is simply sexual intercourse outside of marriage.
7. *ho tropos*—Way, manner, guise, kind, manner of life, character, conduct, life-style.
8. *aphilarguros*—Not greedy, not loving money.

the present things; for He Himself has said: I will never desert you, neither will I ever forsake you.

6   So that we say with confidence,[9]

> The Lord *is* a helper to me, and I will not fear;
> What shall man do to me?

7   Keep in mind your leaders[10] (those who spoke to you the word of God), observing closely the outcome of their way of life; keep on imitating[11] their faith.

8   Jesus Christ *is* the same[12] yesterday, and today and forever.

9   Be not carried away by diverse and strange[13] teachings; for *it is* good that the heart be strengthened by grace—not by foods,[14] wherein they who so lived were not helped.

10   We have an altar[15] from which those serving the tabernacle have no right to eat.

11   For the bodies of those animals[16] whose blood is brought into the holy place by the high priest *as a sacrifice* for sin are burned outside the camp.

12   Wherefore Jesus also, that He might sanctify the people through His own blood, suffered outside the gate.[17]

---

9. *tharrountas*—From *tharreō*, be courageous, be confident, bold.

10. *hēgoumenōn*—Present middle participle, your leaders, those who proclaim to them the message of God's word.

11. *mimeisthe*—From *mimeomai*, which in turn comes from *mimos*, mimic, actor. Keep on imitating their faith.

12. *ho autos*—The same, that is, unchanging in character.

13. *xenais*—From *xenos*, foreign, strange, unheard of, surprising.

14. *brōmasin*—By food, a reference to the Jewish ritualistic rules about meats.

15. *thusiastērion*—Altar, that is, the Christians who have a spiritual altar, not the literal altar, as did the ritualistic priests of the old covenant. This reference harks back to 7:13.

16. *zōōn*—From *zōon*, a living being or thing (not human), animal, living creatures. The only case in the New Testament or in the LXX where this word is used of a sacrificial victim (Robertson).

17. *exō tēs pulēs*—From *pulē*, literally the gate of a city, hence outside the city gate.

13   So, let us keep on going out there to Him,[18] outside the camp, bearing His reproach.

14   For we have not here a permanent city, but we keep on striving for[19] the One that is to come.

15   Through Him,[20] then, let us keep on offering up a sacrifice of praise continually to God, that is the fruit of lips[21] that praise His name.

16   But the doing of good and sharing, forget not;[22] for with such sacrifices God is well pleased.

17   Follow your leaders, and submit[23] to them, for these keep watch over your souls as they shall give account, that with joy they may do this, and not complaining[24]—for this *would be* unprofitable for you.

18   Keep on praying for us, for we are persuaded that we have a good conscience,[25] desiring to conduct ourselves commendably in all things.

---

18. *exerchōmetha pros auton*—Let us keep on going out there to Him . . . a challenge to follow Christ no matter what the cost.

19. *epizētoumen*—From *epizēteō*, strive for, seek after, search for, wish for. The "abiding city" is yet to come!

20. *di' autou*—Through Him, that is, through Christ.

21. *karpon cheileōn*—Fruit of lips. This explains the character of "a sacrifice of praise," and Christians are to keep on offering up such sacrifices, for Christ is a living Lord.

22. *mē epilanthanesthe*—Forget not. The sacrifice of praise is good, and proper, but there is a practical side to Christianity that must not be neglected; namely, "the doing of good and fellowship."

23. *hupeikete*—From *hupeikō*, to give up, yield, submit to the authority of another.

24. *mē stenazontes*—From *stenazō*, to groan, sigh, complain, hence, uncomplaining.

25. *kalēn suneidēsin*—Good conscience. From *suneidēsis*, consciousness, conscience, conscientiousness, moral consciousness. If the conscience is not "good" *(kalēn)*, it can lead one astray. The conscience to be good has to have the impact of Christian instruction and divine motivation.

19   And *the* more exceedingly I entreat you to do this that I may be restored[26] to you soon.

XX. Benediction and Salutations (13:20-25)

20   Now the God of the peace,[27] who brought up from the realm of the dead our Lord Jesus, the great shepherd of the sheep with the blood of an eternal covenant,

21   make you complete[28] in every good thing to do His will,[29] doing in us that which is well pleasing in His sight, through Jesus Christ; to whom *be* the glory for ever and ever. Amen.

22   But I entreat you, brothers, bear with[30] the word of the exhortation, for I have also written to you briefly.

23   Know ye that our brother Timothy has been set free,[31] with whom, if he come soon, I shall see you.

24   Greet[32] all your leaders and all the saints. They of Italy greet you.

25   The grace[33] *be* with you all.

---

26. *apokatastathō*—From *apokathistēmi*, restore, bring back, give back, reestablish.

27. *tēs eirēnēs*—The peace, the peace of God, God's peace, the peace that only God can bring. See Philippians 4:7. See Caudill, *Philippians: A Translation with Notes*, p. 24, note 5.

28. *katartisai*—From *katartizō*, prepare, put in proper condition, complete, restore, put in order, make complete.

29. *to thelēma autou*—The will of Him, His will.

30. *anechesthe*—From *anechō*, endure, put up with, bear with, in the sense of "hear willingly" (Bauer).

31. *apolelumenon*—From *apoluō*, release, set free, pardon, dismiss, send away. In this case, possibly release from prison in Rome, if he came there at Paul's request (2 Tim. 4:11,21).

32. *aspasasthe*—From *aspazomai*, to greet, salute, pay respects to as in Acts 25:13.

33. See footnote 25 in chapter 4.

EXPLANATORY NOTES

CHAPTER 1

The opening verses of the epistle (1:1-4) present an excellent summary of the main theme of the epistle. All previous revelation was preparatory and fragmentary. In Christ, the revelation is absolute. Without the customary salutation, and with no mention of author or destination, the writer set forth his premise in sonorous words. The chaste style of the Greek reflects a measure of refinement of which any writer could be justly proud. The theme of verses 1 and 2 is God. The theme of verses 3 and 4 is God's Son. Verse 4 introduces the theme of the rest of the chapter.

● 1   Verse a emphasizes the fragmentary character of previous revelation. But the writer in no way denigrated the revelation of the Old Testament that came by way of Noah, Abraham, Moses, David, and the prophets. God spoke to them, and through them, in various manners—by signs, dreams, and visions; but the revelation was always fragmentary and incomplete. This incompleteness was due not to God's inability but rather to man's incapacity, at the time, to receive the fuller revelation.[1] The writer did not deal in specifics as to the previous revelation. In the words of Peter: "For no prophecy ever came by the will of man: but men spake from God, being moved by the Holy Spirit" (2 Pet. 1:21, ASV).

Note the absence of argument in these opening verses for the existence of God. That was assumed by the writer. "Since the essential nature of God is love, he can do no other than manifest himself to those who believe in him.

"God is not discovered; he reveals himself."[2]

The seat of honor to a king was on his right hand (1 Kings 2:19).

● 2   Verse 2 emphasizes the finality of the revelation of the Son, together with the character of His inheritance (*whom He made heir of all things*) and His creative activity *(through whom also He made the worlds)*. Christ's role in creation was a primal conviction of the early Christians. He was, to them, the agent of God in creation.

● 3   Here the writer deftly painted an arresting portrait of the Son. He is "the radiance" of the glory of God. The word *glory (doxēs)* was used to signify the manifest presence of the Lord. It was used, for instance, of the pillar of fire to signify God's guiding presence with the Israelites in the Exodus. It was likewise "identified either with the ark of the covenant or with the column of fire or smoke over the altar."[3] (See 1 Sam. 4:21-22; Ezek. 1:28.) This can mean that He was the effulgence, the light itself, or light of God that is reflected; or it can mean that the Son was the radiant splendor of God. Moreover, the Son is presented as the inherent *character* of God's entire person. The word *character (charaktēr)*, which originally signified the mark left by the engraver's tool, came to represent a distinguishing peculiarity or an exact reproduction. The word in the ancient Greek also meant a *seal* or *impression* or *mark* left on the wax by the seal.[4] The word is also found in the inscriptions for "person" and for "exact reproduction" of a person.[5]

Well might Jesus say, "He that hath seen me hath seen the Father" (John 14:9). Christ's powerful character is marked by His relationship to the universe which He "sustains . . . by the word of His power." Christ was not only active in creation, but He also continues to be active in sustaining the universe which He created. The word *pherōn,* variously translated, "bears up," "upholding," might best be translated by the word *sustains* from the old Latin word *sustinerēre* "to hold up, sustain, give support or relief to, supply with sustenance, nourish, etc." This is what Christ does for the whole universe of man's existence. The writer also showed His redemptive activity, for it was by Him that "purification from sins" was achieved. Note how the argument for Christ's superiority proceeds: the cleansing *of* sins (generally) or the cleansing *from* sins (with reference to persons) prepares the way for the argument of Christ's superiority over angels. His is the only name given among men whereby salvation comes to sinners. Last of all, the writer depicted His supreme exaltation as Savior and Redeemer for it is He, and not another, who sits "on the right hand of the Majesty on high," whereby He continues His mediatorial work as Savior and Redeemer. Christ did not stand, as angles are usually represented (1 Kings 22:19); neither did He fall on His face in God's presence or cover His eyes as did the seraphs in Isaiah's vision (Isa. 6:2), but with dignity He took His seat at the right hand of God. The words *the Majesty,* of course, refer to "the majesty of God." Such words were used by Jews and Christians alike to avoid "unnecessary possibilities for blasphemy"—words like "Power" (Matt. 26:64), "the throne of the Majesty" (Heb. 8:1), "the Holy One," etc.[6]

● 4   Here the writer began to develop the argument for the superiority of Christ over angels, inasmuch as He has inherited a name "more excellent than they." Shown in 1:2 as superior to the prophets, He is also shown to be superior to angels (1:4 to 2:18). The verb used is perfect active indicative meaning that he inherited the name and continues to have it. It is no passing thing. According to ancient Jewish beliefs, angels were "the beings who are the instruments in the bringing of God's word and the working of God's will in the universe of men. They are, as it were, the go-betweens, the liaison officers, between God and man. They were said to be spirits who were made of an ethereal fiery substance like blazing light."[7] Neither eating nor drinking nor begetting children, they were regarded as "immortal" and a "kind of entourage, the *familia,* of God."[8] Constant in their attendance to the throne of God, they shared in the counsels of God. Nameless at first, the Jews began to assign the angels names such as Gabriel, Raphael, Phanuel. Essentially, as the word *angel* (*aggelos*) indicates, angels were regarded as messengers of God to men, and some were supposed to preside over various aspects of nature. Even little children experienced their guarding care.

With this background of angelology, it is easy to sense the necessity for the writer to deal with the Son in relation to angels and to prove His superiority over them; else Christ's role as God's intermediary might grow pale in men's belief alongside that of the angels. And the real danger in the traditional concept of angels lay in the fact that they, rather than the Son, might be looked upon as the Christian's chief advocate with God. The word *name* (*onoma*) as used here conveys the "oriental sense of rank."[9] The word *inherited,* in the light of ancient usage, might be translated "obtained" or "acquired." (See other names attributed to Christ, names like Son, King, bright and Morning Star, Lily of the valley, the Good Shepherd, the Light of the world, the Bread of life.)

By virtue of His sonship, His creative relationship to the worlds, His radiant character, His sustaining relationship to the universe, His effective mission as Redeemer from sin, and His position of dignity and power "on high," Christ has become "so much better" and much "more excellent" than the angels. He alone enjoys the position of authority and privilege accorded only to the Son, for, after all, angels are only "ministers or servants in the realm of God's creation."[10]

● 5   In the first quotation that follows (Ps. 2:7), the writer drew upon a passage that was generally regarded as messianic and applied it to Christ as the fulfillment of the critical fact of the messianic longings of Jewish history. No angel was ever referred to by God as his "Son." The thrust of the passage embraces the incarnation of Christ in all of its aspects from the annunciation made to the virgin Mary to the resounding heavenly chorus on the night of the Savior's birth. The voice of heavenly proclamation concerning His sonship is referred to in Mark 1:11 and Luke 9:35. (See also Matt. 17:5 and Rom. 1:4.)

Some would say that the messianic title "Son" was used in the Old Testament when not referring to the Messiah, but the word is never so used in the Old Scriptures.[11] Angels are spoken of in the Psalms as "sons of God" only in reference to them as a body (Ps. 29:1; 89:6); never is a given angel referred to as "son of God." Even so, the nation Israel was referred to as "son" (Hos. 11:1; Ex. 4:22), but no individual Jew was called "son." There is one exception in which Solomon was referred to "as the type of Him who should come after."[12] Some think the words *this day (sēmeron)* indicates by its full character the inauguration of Christ's divine sovereignty which was validated by His resurrection from the dead and His ascension (Acts 13:33; Rom. 1:4; 6:4). Nowhere else in the epistle in the title "Father" used of God. Some refer the words *have I begotten thee* to Christ's incarnation.

● 6   The words *when He shall have brought the firstborn into the world* may refer either to Christ's second coming or to His incarnation, depending upon the meaning and relationship assigned to the word *again (palin)*. Some hold that it appears more logical to refer the words *when He shall have brought* to the second coming of our Lord. For the word *firstborn,* see Psalm 89:27. In Colossians 1:15 the term is used for Christ with reference to His relation to the universe whereas in Romans 8:29 and Colossians 1:18, it is used of his relationship to believers. The term is likewise used to mark Christ's relationship to Mary (Luke 2:7).

● 7   The words *make His angels winds* can be interpreted to mean either "making winds His messengers" (angels) or "making His messengers out of winds," but the latter interpretation seems to be preferable.

The variable character of the mission of angels is further represented in the words *His servants a flame of fire.* However one takes the meaning of the above words, there are times when the proclamation of God's Word assumes the character of "a wind-storm or a fire."[13] Moreover, the mission of God's angels is to worship and serve Him "in the full sense of worship, not mere reverence or courtesy."[14]

"The angels are subject to constant change, He has a dominion for ever and ever; they work through material powers, He—the Incarnate Son—fulfills a moral sovereignty and is crowned with unique joy."[15]

● 8   This quotation is from Psalm 45:6 *ff.* where the reference is to "A Hebrew nuptial ode *(epithalamium)* for a king treated here as Messianic."[16] Here again, there is ambiguity. The words *Thy throne, O God* can be interpreted to mean "God is thy throne" or "Thy throne is God."[17] Either way the words are taken they make good sense. The word *scepter (hrabdos)* is used for staff or walking stick as in Hebrews 11:21. The kingdom of the Messiah is not only divine but also eternal, and the administration of the kingdom is marked by uprightness.

● 9   This quotation (Ps. 45:7) is a continuation of the quotation of the preceding verse. Here is a divine affirmation that the Son is not only characterized by eternal holiness but also represented as positive in His response to righteousness and lawlessness. He "loved" righteousness, and He "hated" lawlessness. His love for righteousness was the *agapē* kind of love that marked God's gift of His Son to the world (John 3:16). His hatred for lawlessness was so great and His desire to see a way provided for mankind to overcome lawlessness that He "suffered for sins once, the righteous for the unrighteous, that he might bring us to God; being put to death in the flesh, but made alive in the spirit" (1 Pet. 3:18).

The word *anointed (echrisen)* is a word from which the verbal noun Christ *(Christos),* the Anointed One, comes. Christ Himself used the same word in His sermon at Nazareth (Luke 4:18): "He anointed me to preach good tidings to the poor." Samuel anointed David, the prototype of Him who was to follow; but the Son, in His incarnate mission, was uniquely God's anointed Son. The words *oil of gladness* perhaps hark back to festive occasions marked by joyful anointing. (See 12:2 and Luke 1:44 for similar occasions of rejoicing.) In comparison with other anointings, however, God's anointing of His Son was "beyond" *(para)* that which any of His partners had ever received.

● 10-12   Here the quotation comes from Psalm 102:25-27. The word *Lord* (*Kurie*), found in the LXX but not in the ancient Hebrew, further accents the character of the Son. The word *Lord* (*Kurios*), Latin *Dominus*, was used to designate an owner of property, more especially slaves (*douloi*), and therefore master and lord (see 1 Pet. 3:6). The term was used of Roman emperors such as Nero. Here the reference is to the creative work of the Son and His triumph over all things. He (Lord) laid the foundation of the earth which, as of all things material, is perishable.

Scientists have much to say concerning heavenly bodies, but so far as we know, none of them holds the heavenly bodies to be eternal in existence. But that of the Son is eternal for He is both the Creator and the Preserver of the universe (John 1:1-3; Col. 1:14 *ff.*). As a worn-out garment, they shall "become old" and "perish," but the Son remains. His existence is eternal. He is unlike garments that become old and are rolled up and put away "as a cloak." He will never change in His character, for He is ever "the same yesterday and to-day, *yea* and for ever" (Heb. 13:8). The Son's years will not come to an end. The expression *will not end* comes from the same verb that was used by Luke (23:45) when He described the failing of the sun when darkness came over the whole land in the sixth to the ninth hour at the crucifixion of Jesus. All nature is subject to the power of the sun, but the Son is subject to nothing except His relationship to the Father.

● 13-14   The seventh quotation comes from the messianic Psalm (110:1), further proof of the superiority of the Son to angels.[18] He is the Son of God who sits at God's right hand in a position of dignity and honor never accorded an angel. Here the sixfold comparison of the Son to the angels comes to a close. They are merely God's servants and heirs of His salvation, whereas Jesus Christ is: Son (v. 5); worshiped by the angels themselves (v. 6); King (v. 8); the Anointed One (v. 9); Creator (vv. 10-12); Ruler (verses 13 *ff.*).

What is more, all "ministering spirits" are "sent forth repeatedly, from time to time as occasion requires" (present passive participle of *apostellō*).[19] Not so of the Son. He was not repeatedly "sent out" but came at the appointed time in the complete fulfillment of prophecy. And He is coming again in behalf of the consummation of our final salvation that is to be experienced by all believers in the last day. All of us who are born of the Spirit came into the possession of salvation at the time of the new birth; but while on earth we continue to grow, to develop, and to work out our individual relationship to that salvation which we will experience in its perfect consummation at His return.

In Christ, therefore, we have the perfect expression of the human-divine relationship. There is nothing partial or temporary about Him. He is the revelation that is final and complete in all its ways.

With the coming of Jesus and the demonstration of His eternal love for humanity, as realized in the atonement, we henceforth came to have direct access to God. No longer need we seek the aid of ministering angels to usher us into the majesty of God's courts above.

As Savior, Redeemer, and Cleanser from sin, Jesus obtained a name that is above every name.

Notes

1. Herschel H. Hobbs, *Studies in Hebrews* (Nashville, Tenn.: Sunday School Board, SBC, 1954), p. 15.
2. Ibid., p. 13.
3. George Wesley Buchanan, *To the Hebrews* (Garden City, N.Y.: Doubleday and Company, Inc., 1972), p. 6.
4. William Barclay, *The Letter to the Hebrews* (Philadelphia: The Westminster Press, 1957), p. 5.
5. A. T. Robertson, *Word Pictures in the New Testament*, vol. 5 (Nashville, Tenn.: Sunday School Board of the SBC, 1931), p. 336.
6. Buchanan, p. 8.
7. Barclay, p. 8.
8. Ibid., p. 9.
9. Robertson, p. 337.
10. Philip E. Hughes, *A Commentary on the Epistle to the Hebrews* (Grand Rapids, Mich.: William B. Eerdmans Publishing Company, 1977), p. 51.
11. Brooke Foss Westcott, *The Epistle to the Hebrews: The Greek Text with Notes and Essays* (New York: MacMillan and Company, 1889), p. 20.
12. Ibid.
13. Robertson, p. 339.
14. Ibid., p. 338.
15. Westcott, p. 26.
16. Robertson, p. 339.
17. Ibid.
18. Marcus Dods, "The Epistle to the Hebrews," *The Expositor's Greek Testament*, vol. 4 (New York: George H. Doran Company, [n.d.]), p. 257.
19. Ibid., p. 341.

CHAPTER 2

Having introduced his readers to the fragmentary and partial character of the former revelation, and having presented God's Son as the full and final revelation, being superior to angels and all previous instruments of revelation, the writer began a series of exhortations that continue throughout the epistle.

● 1   Here the writer included himself ("we") as the subject of the admonition and apparently intended for it to embrace all who had heard the gospel message. But the core of the problem lies not on the part of hearers drifting away from the things they have heard but rather that of being "swept away" by the vicious current of contemporary society. The meaning of the passage depends on the interpretation given to the word *pararuōmen* which, in the active voice, means "to glide by, flow (as a river) by or past." But the verb form is second aorist passive subjunctive, which indicates an action that is actually happening to the subject in question. Dr. Edward A. McDowell translated the passage, "'Lest perchance *we be drifted by*,' or *we be flowed by*."[1] Persons, coming under the influence of godless culture and the pressure of non-Christian concepts of truth and duty, can so yield to the pressure that they are literally "swept away" from the ideal by the currents of circumstance. Here is a stirring commentary on contemporary society. Many so-called Christians seem to be gradually losing the ability to distinguish between the things that differ—to tell right from wrong. This may be the gravest and most threatening aspect of the Christian life-style today.

● 2-3   "For if . . . " Here the writer introduced a condition which, by the words employed, is assumed as true. The reference to angels apparently alludes to Acts 7:38,53; Galatians 3:19. If these acts of disobedience against the word "spoken through the angels" received "a just penalty," how shall "we escape," we who have neglected "so great salvation" as that first spoken through the Lord and also confirmed by those who heard? The Lord Jesus is superior to angels; and His message, the new and superior revelation, is full and complete, not partial, not fragmentary. The certainty of retribution, brought out here, was to be considered on the basis of the authority of the one revealing the message. The angels were regarded as organs of divine communication, but the message of Jesus is superior, and when His message of salvation is deliberately disregarded the consequences are even more grave. The Lord Jesus was the direct Messenger of the Father, and there is no way for one to disregard His message with impunity. Both words *transgression* and *disobedience (parabasis kai parakoē)* use the prefix *para* as does the word *pararuōmen* (swept away, flowed by) and indicate a "stepping aside," a "neglect to obey." Those who heard Jesus were only a generation away, but remember Paul himself "got his message directly from Christ"[2] (Gal. 1:11).

The reference of the sins of the fathers in the wilderness which cut them off from the privilege of entering the Promised Land does not mean that they were lost in our traditional sense of the word *lost*. They were lost to their generation, all right, and were not allowed to enter the Promised Land as did Joshua and Caleb and the younger ones. This "so great salvation" refers to the total redemption of sinful man. It embraces not only the initial experience where one, by adoption, becomes a child of God; it also has to do with the continuing salvation experience while in the flesh together with the ultimate realization of the salvation that is to be revealed at the last day. A person may be saved, "yet so as through fire," with his works destroyed (1 Cor. 3:13-15).

● 4   In bypassing the message first spoken by the Lord Jesus and confirmed by those who heard it, they disregarded the witness of God Himself who joined with them in giving additional testimony by means of signs and wonders and various distributions of the Holy Spirit as He saw fit to do so. The writer used the instrumental case with the words *signs* and *powers* and *distributions* of the Holy Spirit and, as Robertson emphasized, each word "adds an idea about the *erga* (works) of Christ."[3] There was no shortage of testimony, even of additional testimony, and those who neglected the great salvation were wholly without excuse. They had "signs" to convince them of the credibility of the witness. They beheld "wonders" and looked upon "powers" and amazing demonstrations of power by the Holy Spirit; yet apparently some of them were on the verge of being swept away by the swirling waters of the rivers of circumstance.

● 5   Now the writer began to deal at length with the humanity of Jesus (2:5-18), the Son of man and showed how, in this respect, He is superior to angels. Bluntly, he said that it was "not unto angels" that God subordinated "the world to come," that is, the new order, the salvation of which the gospel message speaks. Christ introduced this new order rather than the angels and in doing so rendered "obsolete the old dispensation of rites and symbols."[4] Christ is the mediator of the new order, the intermediary, the absolute full and final revelation of its character and purpose. It is all in His charge and not in the charge of angels.

● 6-8   Next, the writer graphically portrayed the frailty of humanity. There is a Jewish tradition that these words were addressed to God by the ministering angels when Moses was on the mount to receive the law: "O Lord of the world . . . wilt Thou give to flesh and blood that precious thing which Thou hast kept for 974 generations? . . . Give Thy glory rather to heaven" (Sabb, 88, I).[5] The picture is that of humanity according to God's intention rather than a picture of what we in reality are. By creation, God had in mind for humanity a destiny that includes the complete mastery over nature. It was to this end that He was concerned for our future and visited us. But humanity fell tragically short of this ideal. We proved ourselves unworthy of the universal sovereignty intended for us by God; but the picture remains "not yet"—"now we see not yet all things subjected to him" (v. 8). With the fall of humanity, our partnership with God was altered. No longer did we have dominion over nature. Nor does humanity have dominion over nature today although we have achieved marvelous progress in the realm of material things. Neither the moon landing, nor the staggering inquiries into space, nor the splitting of the atom, is able to bring back the full measure of our intended sovereignty under God. Whatever we achieve of the original intent of God with reference to our spiritual destiny can only be realized through our redemptive relationship with God in Christ Jesus. "Man's sovereignty was meant to be all-inclusive including the administration of 'the world to come.'"[6] But alas, our failure is evident on every hand.

● 9   *But we do see Jesus,* notwithstanding the frailty of humanity and our tragic failure to realize the full intent of God's glorious purpose for us, "crowned with glory and honor" (v. 9), with the glory and honor that is complete and inviolate. Jesus had to pay a price in order to become mankind's Redeemer. He had to become incarnate and invade the plane of human history and, being representative of humanity, by His incarnation, He was made for a little while "lower than the angels" (v. 7). It was necessary for Him to have this bitter experience, for only through "the suffering of death" could He "taste death in behalf of every one." We should emphasize that His death was *effectual* "in behalf" of everyone but *effective* for persons only as they turn to Him by faith. Herein lay the motive for the incarnation and the sufferings on the cross. In this way Jesus has become the one "through whom the promise to man has been fulfilled and is in fulfillment; while the revelation of the complete fulfillment belongs to the 'world to come.'"[7] In reality, "the words of the Psalm have received a new fulfillment. The Son of God has assumed the nature in which man was created. In that nature—bearing its last sorrows—He has been crowned with glory. The fruit of His work is universal."[8] And herein lies the assurance that man, in the end, will regain his sovereignty; so, while the atoning death of Christ is still in effect for all people, for many it is not yet effective.

● 10-13   This passage has to do not only with the "Son" but also with "many sons." Because of His unique role as Son of God, it was "fitting" for Him whose mission was to lead "many sons unto glory, to make perfect the founder of their salvation through sufferings" (v. 10). Although the Son was already crowned with "glory and honor" and "for whom are all things and through whom are all things," it was necessary for Him to identify with the "many sons" whom He would lead "unto glory." Thus the necessity for the humanity of Jesus, for only by His sufferings could He become the perfect Savior and enter fully into His redemptive mission for humanity. In character, Jesus was already perfect, but by His suffering He received fitness for His redemptive mission. Being completely without "moral imperfection," Jesus "lived his human life in order to be able to be a sympathizing and effective leader in the work of salvation."[9] In this way Jesus became the perfect *pioneer,* the fitting *leader* and *author* and *founder* of the salvation of the many sons and daughters in their quest for full and complete realization of their destiny under God.

The identity of this relationship in Christ Jesus (v. 11) is further expressed in the words *for both the one who sanctifies and those being sanctified are all of one.* The emphasis on the sanctification here is that of a "process" where there is continuity, the ultimate identity lying in the relationship of the Father to the Son for they are "all of one," referring, of course, "to God as the Father of Jesus" as well as of the "many sons" (v. 10).[10] (See also v. 14 for an extension of the same idea.) In this identifying relationship, Jesus is "not ashamed" to call us, His children, brothers.

The quotation in verse 12 is from Psalm 22:22. The word *congregation* (*ekklēsias*), a term used in ancient Greek for "assembly" of citizens and among the early Hebrews for the children of Israel, came to be used for the local church and also for the church in general or for the kingdom (Matt. 16:18; Heb. 12-23).[11] The picture is that of the Messiah sharing with others in public worship just as Jesus did during the days of His incarnation.

In verse 13 the Messiah is portrayed as "putting his trust in God" just as others do. This, we know, Jesus did throughout the days of His incarnation. The "togetherness" that is so marked in the relationship of the Son to the many sons is clearly indicated in verses 11-13. Glorious indeed is the writer's portrayal of the unity of Jesus with humanity in the course of human redemption and of our mission on earth as followers of the Christ.

● 14-15   In that the children have shared "in blood and flesh" (a reference that harks back to the prophet Isaiah and his children which "foreshadowed Christ and His children"),[12] the sharing of the fellowship of "the Son" and "the sons" became complete.

But more was accomplished than this: by His death, the Son brought "to naught him that has the power of death, that is, the devil." The sting of death was removed by Christ though death is not yet brought "to naught." People still die. But while believers are still subject to death, *per se,* the terrors of death are gone. Christ has removed them. The last enemy, said Paul, that is to be destroyed is death itself, and that will come at the return of our Lord.

But the one having power over death, that is, the devil, has lost his power. In Christ's resurrection from the grave, even as He had promised, death lost its sting.

Moreover, in Christ's victory over the prince of death (v. 14), those in "fear of death throughout all their lifetime" (v. 15) were delivered from that fear. No longer were they "subject to slavery" (v. 15). Mankind's fear of death reflected Satan's power over death, and the prince of death was overcome by Jesus by means of His own death and resurrection. Here we come to the heart of the purpose of the incarnation which is further expressed in the freedom that came to people by faith through His death, burial, and resurrection. Until His victory, people "throughout all their lifetime, were subject to slavery" (v. 15). They were "held in," "bound to" fear—literally "bond-slaves of fear."[13]

Now Jesus could say, "I am the resurrection, and the life" (John 11:25).

● 16   As though to strengthen the premise that has just gone before, the writer said, "for surely" (that is, "of course") "it is not angels that He is helping but the descendants of Abraham that He is helping" (v. 16). Herein lies the complete identification of the Son with the sons who are the descendants of Abraham. Christ initiated a new order. God's final plan of redemption was projected through Him. He was the author, the pioneer, the founder of the plan.

● 17   Here is revealed the heart of the mission of Jesus: first it was necessary for Him to be identified with His brothers in suffering and in death so that "He might become a merciful and faithful High Priest in things relating to God." His mission was undertaken voluntarily (John 10:17), and to accomplish redemption (John 3:16). He was "under obligation to be properly equipped for that priestly service and sacrifice."[14] Here the writer introduced the theme of the epistle, namely, "Jesus as the priest-victim."[15] The words *merciful* and *faithful* characterize Jesus in His role as High Priest. This stands in sharp and tragic contrast with the Sadducean high priests such as Caiphas and Annas who were little more than ecclesiastical tools and puppets. Though aligned with Rome, the high priest alone could enter the holy of holies to officiate in behalf of his own sins and the sins of the people. Jesus had no sin and officiates only in behalf of the sins of others—and that with mercy and fidelity.

In being fully human, as well as fully God, and having suffered and been tempted just as we suffer and are tempted, and that on His part without sin, Jesus became "able" to accomplish His mission as Redeemer . . . "able to run to the cry of those who are being tempted" (AT), and to give each one who comes to Him for help the needed assistance.

By means of His complete identification with humanity, both in life and in death, and by His resurrection from the dead, Jesus did these four things: "(1) he destroyed the work of the devil, v. 14; (2) he delivered his children from the fear of death, v. 15; (3) he became a merciful high priest, v. 17; (4) he became a helper of the tempted, v. 18."[16]

Notes

1. Herschel H. Hobbs, *Studies in Hebrews* (Nashville, Tenn.: Sunday School Board, SBC, 1954), p. 19.
2. A. T. Robertson, *Word Pictures in the New Testament,* vol. 5 (Nashville, Tenn.: Sunday School Board, SBC, 1931), p. 343.
3. Ibid.
4. Ibid., p. 344.
5. Brooke Foss Westcott, *The Epistle to the Hebrews: The Greek Text with Notes and Essays* (New York: MacMillan and Company, 1889), p. 43.
6. Robertson, p. 345.
7. Westcott, p. 45.
8. Ibid., p. 44.
9. Robertson, p. 347.
10. Ibid., p. 348.
11. Ibid.
12. Westcott, p. 52.
13. Robertson, p. 349.
14. Ibid., p. 350.
15. Ibid.
16. *The Broadman Bible Commentary,* vol. 12 (Nashville, Tenn.: Broadman Press, 1972), p. 28.

CHAPTER 3

The premise of the writer of the Epistle to the Hebrews, from beginning to end, is the supremacy of Jesus Christ in all things relating to God. He Himself is the full and complete revelation of God, and only through Him, as Mediator and Friend, can we have direct access to God. Already the writer had shown that Christ is superior to the prophets in that all former revelation was partial and fragmentary, whereas in Jesus Christ divine revelation is full and final. The writer then showed the superiority of Jesus to the angels who, likewise, are ministering servants but without the unique mission and position of honor accorded Jesus as God's only Son. The use of the human name (Jesus) of the Lord called to mind a chief problem of the Hebrews, namely, the Lord's humanity.[1] Now the writer proved the superiority of Jesus to Moses. There was good reason in doing this, for Moses himself was unique among the prophets. God spoke to him face-to-face on the mountain when He delivered to him the law of God— the Ten Commandments. To think of Moses was to think of the law, and at least one Jewish teacher, Rabbi Jose ben Chalafta of the second century, held that God ranked Moses higher than the ministering angels.[2] "The voice from heaven to Moses was an earthly calling, a calling to the fulfilment of an earthly life," and the calling of the Christian is "a calling to a life fulfilled in heaven, in the spiritual realm."[3] "The bond of union lies in that which is shared and not in the persons themselves."[4]

● 1-6   The expression *holy brothers* is found only here in the New Testament. The writer's appeal is directly to the body of believers whose lives, presumably, had been set apart unto God for His use and unto His glory. What is more, they are sharers (partakers) of a calling that came from heaven and that beckons them to heaven. The words *fix your mind on (katanoēsate)* convey the thought of bringing the mind to the point that it *rests upon* Jesus and *finds rest in* Him. We have a similar colloquialism in English, "Keep your mind on it." With Jesus, the search is over. The final revelation has come. In this relationship the mind is to be firm, stable, unyielding, and unending. After all, Jesus is *the* Apostle of God the Father. Only here in the New Testament is Jesus called an Apostle. The word literally means "one who is sent forth." Used of the envoys of the Sanhedrin, it was a familiar term to the Jews. The *apostoloi* of the Sanhedrin were those sent out as authoritative bearers of commands. On their missions they represented the voice of the king and country of their mission. But Jesus was more than the Apostle who came straight from God, clothed with power, and with the authority to speak His words: He was also *the* High Priest. As the Latin word for priests suggests (*pontifex*—bridge builder), Jesus became the perfect Mediator between human beings and God. Being both human and divine, perfect man and perfect God, Jesus became the one and only door of perfect access to God.

As Apostle and High Priest, Jesus was faithful in carrying out His assignments even as was Moses "in all His [God's] house." Notice the writer never belittled prophets, angels, or Moses but clearly pointed out the superiority of Christ in each case. His faithfulness referred to His perfect humanity with reference to His authoritative and mediatorial office. It should be noted that both Christ and Moses, in their mission, were separate and apart from other divine messengers in that their mission dealt with the divine economy as a whole. While prophets, kings, and priests were delegated to deal with the various aspects of truth, the mission of Christ and Moses had to do with the whole house of God. "The 'house of God' is the organised society in which He dwells. Israel was the type of redeemed mankind."[5] Hence the word *house* as used here in relation to God though essentially one in relation to the mission of Moses and Jesus becomes twofold and thought of in terms of the two agents—Jesus and Moses.

Verses 3 and 4 merely reassert the superiority of Christ reflected in verses 1 and 2; while Moses was only an instrument lost in the economy which was given to him, Jesus Christ was the author of and instituted the economy which was His.[6] The work and position of Moses and of the Mosaic dispensation as a whole was provisional, pointing clearly to an antitype.

What is more, this same Jesus is worthy of more glory than Moses since the builder of the house is greater than the house itself. Notice the terms *glory* *(doxēs)* and *honor (timēn)*. " 'Glory' is internal, as light flashed from an object: 'honor' is external, as light shed upon it."[7]

In verses 5 and 6, the analogy between Moses and the people of God, Christ, and the church is crystal clear. The mission of Moses was that of a servant sent from God to bring instructions and warnings to the people of God and to deliver them from Egypt. But Moses could only speak about God whereas Jesus spoke as God's Son, identifying himself completely with God. "He that hath seen me hath seen the Father; . . . I am in the Father, and the Father in me" (John 14:9-11); "I and the Father are one" (John 10:30). The writer passed from the human title *('Iēsous)* to the "prophetic" title *(Christos).*

Moses was a "testimony" of "things to be spoken later"; Jesus was the one spoken of and dreamed about for centuries before. As Messiah, He became the reality of the things spoken of and which in themselves were merely shadows, harbingers of the things to come. While both Moses and Christ were perfect in their fidelity, Moses was merely "a servant" who administered the affairs of God's house on earth while Christ exercised His fidelity as a Son who was the sovereign over God's house (v. 1-2).

The term *God's house* was frequently used to represent the church (1 Pet. 4:17; 1 Tim. 3:15; 1 Pet. 2:5). Christ spoke of His body of believers as a church (Matt. 16:18) and declared Himself as the builder of the church. And over the church He still presides as its "head" (Col. 1:18). Identifying himself and the Hebrew Christians as a part of the body, the church, the writer, with a brooding note of contingency, reflected more than once in the epistle, "whose house we are, if indeed we hold fast our confidence and the pride of our hope" (v. 6).

In the eyes of the world, the church can have validity and power only in proportion as those who profess to be Christ's followers remain steadfast and immovable in faith and do not continue on in sin since, if His seed dwells in them, they are unable *(dunatai)* to continue on in sin because they are "begotten of God" (1 John 3:9).

● 7-11   Up to this point the writer has dealt with the unique supremacy of Jesus, proving His unique superiority to prophets, to angels, and to Moses. Now the writer began his exhortation for all the followers of Jesus to have unwavering trust in Him and to give to Him absolute obedience. To buttress and clinch his argument, he employed a quotation from Psalm 95:7-11 which clearly portrays the awful consequences of distrust and disobedience on the part of God's people.

According to the writer of the epistle, it is the Christians who now comprise the house of God rather than the Hebrews in the old order. The Christians have access to the fullness of the blessing and the spiritual privileges of God as a part of His household, but the enjoyment of the spiritual privileges is contingent upon the response of the Christian to the glorious hope which the Hebrews were warned against losing.

So, in these verses (7-11), a quotation of Psalm 95:7-11, the peril of apostasy was vividly depicted by the writer as he cited the example of Israel. To better understand the passage, one should read Numbers 13:1 *ff*. which affords a historical background of the rebellion. Israel, through the leadership of Moses, had been delivered from bondage and death in Egypt; but as the people began to undergo the hardships of the desert on the pilgrimage, and had to face up to the report of the twelve spies who were sent out to evaluate the land, they panicked. Only Joshua and Caleb spoke words of faith and encouragement while the people as a whole became as whimpering children, filled with desire to return to Egypt. In fact, the whole congregation lifted up their voices and cried out in protest . . . and the people wept (Num. 14:1-2). Some even wanted to "make a captain" for their return to Egypt (v. 4).

So great was the disappointment of the Lord that He said to Moses, "I will smite them with the pestilence, and disinherit them" (v. 12). And had it not been for the prayer of Moses, that is what would have taken place. But as a result of Moses' prayer and his eloquent petition for mercy God pardoned Israel, and they are still His people. Nevertheless, none of those enrolled above twenty years of age was allowed to enter the Promised Land. They had broken the covenant relation and lost the opportunity to share in the fulfillment of God's purpose which, in spite of Israel's rebellion, was fulfilled through the leadership of Caleb and Joshua. Even Moses was deprived of the privilege of entry into Canaan. Through stubborn unbelief, their contribution to the fulfillment of the purposes of God was at end (v. 11). The Israelites were not satisfied with God's promise, and "demanded objective proof (*erga,* deeds) of God."[8] Somehow, Israel did not understand the ways of God and in their murmurings and exasperations deprived themselves of the supreme joy of entering into the rest (Canaan) which lay just ahead.

● 12-15   In these verses the writer turned to the Hebrew Christians and said to them, in effect: "And you Hebrew Christians of our day are in danger of giving way to the same spirit of distrust and to similar acts of disobedience. You have been saved. There is no question about your redemption. But you are not advancing in Christian stature, and you are failing to demonstrate your total trust in Christ and your unfailing obedience to His commands. You are having trials, and you will have more trials in the days ahead—just as did our forefathers in the wilderness. Some of you are backsliding already, and others are becoming lukewarm in their love for the Lord. And if you are not careful, you will be giving way to the same sort of distrust and acts of disobedience that characterized your forefathers in the desert. This does not mean that you question your salvation, your redemption from past sins. This does not mean that you are disavowing your initial act of faith in receiving Jesus as Savior and Lord. It does mean that you are not exercising the faith you ought to exercise in trusting God to make use of you in the fulfillment of His overall plan for the redemption of the world. It means that you have utterly no faith (*apistia*, literally no faith at all) in God's guidance and protecting care as you face the future. By your lack of faith (which is the very substance of things hoped for), and by your acts of willful disobedience, you may keep God from opening up to you 'the windows of heaven,' and pouring out blessings upon you 'that there shall not be room enough to receive it'! (Mal. 3:10)."

God had a plan for the deliverance of the children of Israel from bondage, slavery, and death in Egypt. That is why He preserved the life of Moses, reared him in the king's court, and prepared him with surpassing knowledge for the Herculean task of becoming the leader of His people. God took him up on the mountain, and spoke to him face-to-face, and delivered to him the tablets containing the ten basic laws to be observed by all the peoples of the earth who desire a viable society. But even Moses was not allowed to enter the Promised Land—another stage in the pilgrimage of the promised *rest*. In a fit of anger and irritation, he failed to *speak* to the rock in the name of the Lord as God commanded but *struck* it. The water came forth all right, but for this single act of disobedience and distrust Moses was not allowed to enter the Promised Land; rather, he was buried alone in Nebo's lonely height, and no one knows his burying place to this day. He, like the children of Israel, in a fiery moment displayed his lack of absolute trust in God, taking things into his own hands for the moment, and failing to hold fast "the pride of our hope."

Moses was God's man. The Hebrews who fell in the wilderness—all above twenty years of age save Caleb and Joshua—were God's people. But they robbed themselves of the glorious privilege of entering the Promised Land. They became petulant, disobedient, and full of disbelief. The Lord said, in effect, "Don't you become as they. Pray for one another and ask God to help you renew your faith in Him so that you may become fruitfully active in the fulfillment of His purpose for you and for the world." It was God's will for Israel that she become "a kingdom of priests, and a holy nation" (Ex. 19:6). But Israel fell short of that goal. The seed of Israel entered the Promised Land. The fulfillment of His purpose was only delayed by the disbelief and acts of disobedience on the part of those who fell in the wilderness.

"God has a purpose for you—the Hebrew Christians of our day—if you will not go astray in the heart but seek to understand God's ways. When trials come, fix your eyes upon Jesus, for He will continue to lead you in the fulfillment of His promises, into the blessings of your pilgrimage on earth, as well as unto the final realization of the fullness of your salvation on the day of days when you will see Christ face-to-face in heaven. Have faith! Don't become like the waves of the sea, wind driven, and tossed!"

This matter of an "evil heart of disbelief," accompanied by the "falling away from the living God," can take place "at any time" and on the part of "any one of you." This danger of *disbelief* and *falling away* was no less a danger to the Hebrews of the epistle than it is to Christians today. The words *falling away* (*apostēnai*) carry the sense of withdrawing from, going away, and literally means "to stand off from, to step aside from."[9] But this *disbelief* and *disobedience* (falling away) does not need to take place. For all Christians (not merely the Hebrews) have Jesus the Apostle and High Priest who is able to go before and blaze the path, having been tempted in all points as we, and yet without sin.

The issue here is not a question of being "lost" in the traditional sense of the term. A person who has been genuinely "born of the spirit" will not be lost. Along with the rebirth comes adoption into the family of God. The born-again Christian is actually a member of the family, of the household, of God. I, for instance, was born a *Caudill,* and I will ever be a *Caudill.* Legally, I could change my name, but by blood I would ever be the same person. The Christian has been transformed by the blood of the Lamb, and by faith he or she has laid hold of the promises of an eternal inheritance: "Blessed be the God and Father of our Lord Jesus Christ, who according to his great mercy begat us again unto a living hope by the resurrection of Jesus Christ from the dead, unto an inheritance incorruptible, and undefiled, and that fadeth not away, reserved in heaven for you, who by the power of God are guarded through faith unto a salvation ready to be revealed in the last time" (1 Pet. 1:3-5).

After all, all Christians are partners of the "heavenly calling," partners of Christ, and in this sense share with Christ in the glory of His mission among the human race. (See Luke 5:7; Heb. 1:9; 3:1; 3:14).

● 16-19   Here the writer merely underscored the exhortation of the preceding verses 12-15. Christians who fail to advance in their faith and knowledge and in their personal understanding of Jesus Christ as Savior and Lord simply are deprived of the enjoyment of the blessings that would come to them through faithfulness and obedience. Absolute trust in Christ is the *absolute* necessity on the part of the Christian who would achieve the stature of the full-grown person in Christ. Absolute *obedience* is a requisite on the part of all of the followers of Christ who would experience triumph in their earthly pilgrimage as well as in the day of the final rewards in heaven. And the glorious thing about God's promise is that it is still "today" for all those who are yet alive. There is yet time to repent, to desist from ways of distrust and disobedience. Vows may be renewed, and life-styles changed to conform to His holy purpose.

After all, God's purpose cannot be thwarted by the perfidies of persons. The actual fulfillment of His purpose may be delayed but never defeated; and the fulfillment will come one day "according to the eternal purpose which he projected in Christ Jesus our Lord, in whom we have freedom of speech and access in confidence through faith in him."[10]

Notes

1. Brooke Foss Westcott, *The Epistle to the Hebrews: The Greek Text with Notes and Essays* (New York: MacMillan and Company, 1889), p. 74.
2. William Barclay, *The Letter to the Hebrews* (Philadelphia: The Westminster Press, 1957), p. 22.
3. Westcott, p. 74.
4. Ibid.
5. Ibid., p. 77.

6. Ibid.

7. Ibid.

8. A. T. Robertson, *Word Pictures in the New Testament,* vol. 5 (Nashville, Tenn.: Sunday School Board, SBC, 1931), p. 357.

9. Ibid., p. 358.

10. R. Paul Caudill, *Ephesians: A Translation with Notes* (Nashville, Tenn.: Broadman Press, 1979), p. 36.

CHAPTER 4

Here the division of the chapters is poor since the first eleven verses of chapter 4 merely reemphasize the tragic facts of Hebrew history with respect to God's promised rest for His people and make clear to all that God's eternal plan of redemption extends "far beyond the historical event of the entry of the Israelites into Canaan under Joshua's leadership."[1]

● 1-9   God's plan of redemption through Jesus Christ His Son embraces the whole world of humanity. Hence, the solemn warning to "be fearful" lest someone, having heard the promise, allows himself to be *swept away* from the promises by the cruel waves of circumstance.

The issue here is the promised rest of God (vv. 1,4,7-9). This conventional usage of the word *rest* slants toward heaven and the blessings of the redeemed. And well may this be, for that is part of the picture. But it is not all of the picture. Actually there are three aspects of the overall meaning of the word *rest* as used in Hebrews. (1) The word *rest* applies to God's rest after His creative activity. (2) The word *rest* is used as it applies to the Promised Land. The Hebrews who came up out of Egypt and died in the wilderness (that is, all of those enrolled above age twenty) are spoken of as not having entered into the rest. They were denied the privilege of entering the Promised Land because of their sins of disbelief and disobedience. Those led across the waters of the Jordan by Joshua did enter into the rest that was theirs in the land of promise. In each of these instances the word used for *rest* is *katapausis* which conveys the idea of "stopping," "causing to rest." In other words, God completed the work of creation on the sixth day and rested on the seventh day, for He had "finished his work which he had made" (Gen. 2:1-3). But not all of God's work was finished with creation. That was only one phase of the realization of His purpose for the human race. God's work continues to go on so that He might continue to mold and make people, His highest form of creation, into His own likeness in character and deed. In truth, one might say God's work was only begun during the six days of creation. That is why Jesus said, "My Father continues to work until now" {*heōs arti*}, "and I keep on working." (John 5:17). God completed one stage of the process in the fulfillment of His purpose for humanity, in the creative activity of the first six days and rested from His labors only to begin to implement the second stage of His eternal purpose for the world, namely, *the incarnation of His Son* to serve as the Lamb of God by whose blood all people may be saved from their sins through faith in Him. (3) Then there remains "a sabbath rest" to which our author alluded in verses 8 and 9. "For if Joshua had given them rest, He (God) would not be speaking later of another day. Consequently, there remains a sabbath rest for the people of God."

This "sabbath rest" was misunderstood by rabbis as is seen by some of the prohibitions they established concerning the use of the sabbath. Luke 6:1 *ff.* tells how Jesus and His disciples were going through the grain fields on the sabbath when the disciples plucked some of the ears and ate, "rubbing them in their hands." As a consequence some of the Pharisees said, "Why do ye that which it is not lawful to do on the sabbath day?" They even criticized Jesus for healing the withered right hand of a man on the sabbath. But Jesus answered them, saying, "The Son of man is lord of the sabbath."

The ancient word used by the writer for "a sabbath rest" is *sabbatismos,* not *katapausis.* The sabbath rest that remains (vv. 6-9) for every follower of Jesus Christ is the rest that comes "from the struggle to attain their destiny in the face of persecution, as God's rest was an end to his work in creation. . . . As God changed his activity from that of creation to redemption, so are the Hebrew Christians in their *sabbatismos* to change their work from that of a struggle to achieve their goal of Christian character into that of becoming partners (3:14) with Christ in redemptive service."[2]

We who are followers of Christ today have the promise of rest just as did the Israelites. Hence, the words *another day* (v. 8), and "a certain day, To-day" (v. 7). "The parallel holds as to the promise, the privilege, the penalty."[3] All who come to Jesus by faith ("we who believed") do "keep on entering into [the] rest" (v. 3). For the indefinite reference "somewhere" (v. 4) to a passage in the Old Testament, see Genesis 2:2.

● 10-11   This does not really mean "cessation of work," but an interlude preceding the next stage of endeavor. Here the writer entreated the Hebrew Christians not to make the same mistake the Hebrews made in the wilderness, and the word translated "let us make every effort" (*spoudasōmen*) also may enjoin haste, zeal, eagerness, in the effort to enter "into that rest." The danger of looking back is always present as well as that of the consequent acts of overt distrust in God and disobedience.

● 12-13   Here is a graphic portrayal of God's power "to penetrate to the centre of a man's personality."[4] Nothing is concealed to God's eyes. To the ancient Jew, God sees everything (Prov. 15:3), and all is naked and bare to His eyes . . . and helpless before Him apart from His grace and mercy.

● 14-15   The Son of God is "great" because He is superior: to the Levitical priesthood (4:14 to 12:3), to the prophets (1:1-3); to the angels (1:4 to 2:18); and to Moses (3:1 to 4:13), serving under a better covenant (8:1-13), with better promises (10:19 to 12:3), a better sacrifice (9:13 to 10:18), and a better sanctuary (9:1-12). Jesus' sinlessness and His ability to sympathize with all who turn to Him, by faith, and to save unto the uttermost set Him apart as a unique Redeemer (v. 15).

● 16   Instead of standing off from Him, "let us make daily use of him,[5] knowing that in Him we will always receive mercy and find grace for timely help.

Notes

1. Philip E. Hughes, *A Commentary on the Epistle to the Hebrews* (Grand Rapids, Mich.: William B. Eerdmans Publishing Company, 1977), p. 155.
2. Herschel H. Hobbs, *Studies in Hebrews* (Nashville, Tenn.: Sunday School Board, SBC, 1954), pp 41-42.
3. A. T. Robertson, *Word Pictures in the New Testament,* vol. 5 (Nashville, Tenn.: Sunday School Board, SBC, 1931), p. 360.
4. Hugh Montefiore, *A Commentary on the Epistle to the Hebrews* (New York: Harper and Row, 1964), p. 88.
5. Robertson, p. 366.

CHAPTER 5

In chapter 5 the writer introduced the doctrine of the Messiah's Melchizedekian priesthood, a view not found in contemporary or earlier Jewish literature nor in other writings of the early church; and as he did so, one thing is obvious: he had an exceptional knowledge of the Scriptures, "sustained by the logical thinking of a forceful and rigorous intellect, and expressed with the elegance and precision of a cultured Hellenist."[1] Already the writer had shown that Jesus was qualified for the high priesthood. Now he went on to show how Jesus fulfilled these qualifications.

● 1-3   Of the qualifications for every high priest of the Levitical order, two were requisite: (1) human compassion and (2) divine appointment (5:4). He must be taken from among men because his mission was to deal with men, and this required human sympathy. Only in this way would he be able "to deal gently with the ignorant and erring ones." The word translated "deal gently" (*metriopathein*) was used by Josephus (*Ant.* XII. 32) to characterize the moderation of both Vespasian and Titus with reference to the Jews.[2]

In the matter of gifts (*dōra*) and sacrifices (*kai thusias*—bloody offerings), he ministered not only in behalf of the sins of the people but also his own sins (7:27). But here the parallelism ends, for Jesus Himself was without sin—for there were no seeds of sin residing in Him that might in themselves produce sin. Still Jesus was thoroughly human just as He was completely divine, and being human He suffered as other persons in ways that brought pain and anguish to His body and mind.

It is easy for a person in high office to become arrogant and to develop an egotistical sense of self-sufficiency. But this state of mind must not take place in the high priest for he himself is plagued with weaknesses "lying around him like a chain."[3] Because of this he is obligated to make an offering for his own sins as well as for those of his people. But Jesus knew no sin though He identified closely with sinners. "Him who knew no sin he made to be sin on our behalf; that we might become the righteousness of God in him" (2 Cor. 5:21).

● **4-6**   Here the writer quoted from Psalm 2:7 to prove the divine appointment of Jesus as High Priest (v. 5), and from Psalm 110:4 to establish the fact of His High Priesthood according to the order of Melchizedek forever (v. 6). Jesus boldly declared that He was sent by the Father on His redemptive mission to the world (John 5:30,43; 8:54; 17:5).

● **7-9**   Verse 7 points out the fact of the sufferings of Jesus in the days of His flesh and how He offered up not *sacrifices* but both "prayers and supplications with strong crying and tears," to the One who was able to deliver Him from the death that lay ahead. Here Satan tried, as during the temptations in the wilderness, to deflect Jesus from His mission as Redeemer—His last attempt at such before Calvary.

God heard His crying and saw His tears in the garden of Gethsemane "because of His reverence *for God*" but still permitted Him to go on in His suffering, so "having been made perfect" He might become for all who look to Him by faith and obey His commands, "the cause of eternal salvation" (v. 9). And in it all Jesus learned obedience (v. 8). The character of the salvation to be enjoyed at the last day by believers will be marked by the character of their obedience to Christ during their days in the flesh. Some will be saved "as by fire"—their works being destroyed.

And just as Christ was *obedient* to the Father, even so through obedience to Him, His followers have access to the *source* of "eternal salvation" (v. 9). At this point, it is well to recall that there are three aspects or emphases in the meaning of the word *salvation (sōtēria)*: the initial step in the process marks the entrance of believers into their role of adoption into the family of God. From that moment on, they are a part of the divine family. They are saved, but as *saved* persons and living under the rainbow of eternal salvation while in the flesh, they have responsibilities that they are to shoulder in working out their own salvation. They are to be obedient to the commands of Jesus and endeavor to manifest in all of their personal interrelationships with others the spirit and mind of Christ (Phil. 2:5).

The words *having been made perfect* (v. 9) (from *teleioō*) are used here not in the sense of our common use of the word *perfect* signifying "freedom from fault." The idea refers rather to the completeness of His preparation as the Author (*founder*) of our salvation (*archēgos*). Through His sufferings and death on the cross whereby He became the Lamb of God making the final sacrifice for the sins of all who would look to Him by faith, all of the prophecies and all of His days of ministry while in the flesh were completed, brought to an end, finished!

● 10   In assuming the role of messianic High Priest, Jesus did so by divine appointment. He was "named" (designated) to the office by God. The honor and the glory of the office was not obtained by Him for Himself (nor was that of Aaron who was also divinely appointed to his office). All other priests, with the exception of Melchizedek, were of the order of Levi. But the writer does not touch on this matter until later.

● 11-14   Westcott titled these verses "Stationariness in religious life and its consequences."[4] As with the physical life of persons, the intellectual and spiritual life—the life of faith—is to experience growth. For the growth to be healthy and strong, there must be exercise in the needed disciplines of growth. One of the problems of the Hebrews had to do with their response to the gospel—they had become "sluggish in hearing." They had misused the opportunities for growth that were theirs during the early period of their discipleship and were satisfied to stop with the "first principles of growth." The foundation had been laid, but they had failed to prepare themselves for the fuller instruction that was to follow. They were still acting like babies when they should have been growing into the stature of full-grown persons in Christ. Instead of becoming teachers (v. 12), they still had need for someone to teach them. They were hardly beyond the kindergarten stage so far as Christian teaching was concerned.

There has been much discussion about the terms *milk (gala)* and *solid food (trophē)*. Some of the early writers regarded the word *milk* as related to the teaching of the young Christians concerning Christ's humanity and "his resurrection and Ascension, while 'the solid food' was the more mysterious teaching on His Godhead."[5] However, the meaning is clarified sufficiently in 6:1 *ff.* The food of babies is *milk,* but the normal food for adults is *solid food.* This vivid contrast between adults and babies is found again in Ephesians 4:13 *ff.* What the writer saw as lacking in his view of the Hebrew Christian was spiritual maturity, both in thought and in deed, as to Christian truth. *By reason of time (dia ton chronon)* the Hebrew Christians should have been disciplined and experienced in the faith, but they were not. "The spiritual maturity of which the apostle speaks is the result of careful exercise. It belongs to those who have their senses—their different organs of spiritual perception—trained, in virtue of their moral state gained by long experience."[6]

Notes

1. Hugh Montefiore, *A Commentary on the Epistle to the Hebrews* (New York: Harper and Row, 1964), p. 96.
2. A. T. Robertson, *Word Pictures in the New Testament,* vol. 5 (Nashville, Tenn.: Sunday School Board, SBC, 1931), p. 367.
3. Ibid., p. 368.
4. Brooke Foss Westcott, *The Epistle to the Hebrews: The Greek Text with Notes and Essays* (New York: MacMillan and Company, 1889), p. 133.
5. Ibid., p. 133 *ff.*
6. Ibid., p. 137.

CHAPTER 6

● 1   Turning from the withering words of rebuke in the closing four verses of chapter 5, the writer, as with a blast of the trumpet shrill and clear, issued a stirring call for advance . . . to emerge from babyhood—from the soft diet of milk to strong food such as an adult would require. "Wherefore"—that is, because of what has just been said, the Hebrew Christians are to leave behind the elementary teaching concerning Christ, and "be borne on to spiritual maturity." The word translated "borne on" (*pherōmetha*) was used in the Pythagorean Schools "in precisely this sense of being borne on to a higher stage of instruction."[1] The Hebrew Christians had continued to toy with the *ABC's* of Christian instruction. The time had come to be "borne on." These "first principles of Christ" or "elementary teaching" should be for the beginners on the Christian pilgrimage. A good foundation is necessary if a building is to rest securely on it, but no one goes on laying a foundation forever. The foundation merely comprises the substructure of the building that is to follow.

Repentance and *faith* comprise the requisite foundation for the Christian life, and there can be no spiritual maturity without such. Actually, one is to be "borne on" but *not away from* faith. The pilgrimage is to reach toward advanced stages of faith, into a deeper and more sustaining faith. Once the foundation of repentance from dead works and faith has been experienced, Christians are to move forward toward spiritual maturity. They are to grow as plants would grow in the natural world. An acorn is not to be an acorn forever. It is to sprout, and grow, and become a strong oak with a trunk and branches that are useful to people. Leave behind the *dead works* ("every sin is a dead work"),[2] and man himself is "dead" as to his spiritual nature, apart from Christ (Rom. 6:23; 7:11), for sin is a death-working principle (Jas. 2:17,26; John 7:25; Rom. 6:1,11; 7:8; Col. 2:13).

● 2   The author mentioned four more of the elementary teachings which, necessary as they are, are not to be dwelt on forever at the expense of progress to Christian understanding and advance in the Christian life-style. The believer is forever to press on toward the achievement of the intended goal of God in Christ. The four elementary teachings are: (1) baptisms, (2) laying on of hands, (3) resurrection of the dead, and (4) eternal judgment. The word *baptisms* as used here does not of itself mean "Christian baptism"[3] but probably also refers to immersions or ablutions practiced in the mystery religions and by the Jewish cults or proselytes, initiates, and worshipers. (See John 3:25.) The "laying on of hands" was a common practice that signified a blessing (Matt. 19:13), healing (Mark 7:32), a symbol of the bestowal of the Holy Spirit (Acts 8:17 *ff.*; 19:6) on ordination, or a separation of an individual for a particular work (Acts 13:3; 1 Tim. 4:14; 5:22; 2 Tim. 1:6). Certainly the resurrection of the dead (whether of the just or unjust) must be understood (1 Cor. 15), and no instruction that bypasses the doctrine of eternal judgment is complete. But elementary instruction and the learning process in Christian experience must pass on to other truths, to a deeper understanding of the concepts of truth and duty as taught by Jesus and by the Bible in general. As Isaac our beloved janitor at First Baptist, Augusta, Georgia, once said to me, "The way I see it, there is no *standstill* in the Christian life. A man's either *going* or *coming.*"

● 3   This verse is rather difficult to explain. Perhaps the words reflect the writer's sense of the overruling purpose of God who is the one who motivates and makes possible all advance, and all instruments of advance. After all, He has the last word in the timing of the stages of the Christian's progress in the quest for spiritual maturity and the ultimate fulfillment of God's eternal purpose in Christ Jesus.

● 4-6   Here we have the setting of one of the battlegrounds of students of Christian doctrine. The followers of John Calvin who, marked by his strong emphasis on the sovereignty of God, dwelt especially on the doctrine of predestination. On the other hand the adherents of Arminius opposed the absolute predestination set forth by strict Calvinism and maintained just as firmly the possibility of salvation for all. Here is the issue: Can a person who has had a genuine Christian experience, being born of the Spirit, ever be lost again?

Before dealing with the answer to this question, it is well to keep in mind the frame of reference. The writer was dealing not with the first aspect of salvation which is merely the initial experience of the believer but rather with aspects of salvation which involve "growth in grace, knowledge, and service."[4] As previously noted, there are three stages in salvation: (1) the initial stage when one is "saved," adopted into the family of God—born from above; (2) the lifelong experience in salvation where you as a Christian continue under the rainbow of promise and, day by day "with reverence and trembling continue to work out your own salvation" (Phil. 2:12-13);[5] (3) the fullness of salvation that is "ready to be revealed in the last time" (1 Pet. 1:5). Some commentators dispose of the problem by regarding the words of the writer to the Hebrews as posing a hypothetical case but a case which represents an impossibility. Still others solve the problem by holding that those who have experienced saving faith and continue steadfast in that faith will never be lost—that such, for them, is an impossibility.

Here again we come back to the example of the Israelites. They had been "saved," for they had been delivered from their bondage in Egypt. But they lost out in the second stage of their salvation experience: they became fretful and murmuring with longings for return to their old abode in Egypt and consequently were deprived of the Promised Land phase of their salvation experience. They died in the wilderness. It was Canaan, their Promised Land experience, that they lost out on. And there was no way on earth for them to be renewed unto that hope, for God had decreed that they must die in the wilderness—the place of their backsliding—while the younger ones went on into the Promised Land and thus experienced the advanced phase of their salvation. Dr. Herschel Hobbs sees clearly the parallel between the Hebrew Christians and the Israelites: "They, too, have had a genuine spiritual experience (vv. 4-5). But they also are faced with the danger of stopping short of their destiny in Christian growth and service by *standing off from* Jesus (3:12). The word translated 'fall away' in verse 6 is *parapesontas* and comes from the Greek verb which carries the root idea of *falling aside* or of deviating from the right path."[6] The word *repentance* (*metanoian,* verse 6) is a much misunderstood word. Basically, it means a *change of mind* "as it appears in one who repents of a purpose he has formed or of something he has done."[7] It is used to mark a change of mind on the part of a person who has begun "to abhor" his misdeeds and errors and has resolved to enter upon a new and better life-style. The verb form *(metanoeō)* occurs in the Septuagint and elsewhere in the sense of "to change one's mind . . . to feel remorse, repent,"[8] to change (Luke 17:3). To me, the word *repent,* in the context of the New Testament, indicates (1) a change of mind—a different way of thinking about right and wrong, (2) a change of heart—a different way of feeling about right and wrong, (3) a change of actions—different conduct, and that for better.

Now in the case of the Israelites who had fallen away, it was impossible to keep on restoring them because they had experienced the passing of religious opportunity so far as entering the Promised Land was concerned. They could not be renewed to that opportunity. They could not be restored to the possibility of that stage of their spiritual maturity. They had been delivered from Egypt, and that deliverance was theirs forever. Still God declared that they had lost their opportunity to enter into the Promised Land—His *rest.* The word commonly translated *crucify afresh (anastaurountas)* does not mean crucify "again" or "afresh" but "up."[9] In classical Greek the word was used in the sense of raising on the cross or crucifying which was followed, as here, with the additional thought of public exposure which was in itself an occasion of disgrace. Of course, the text does not mean that the Hebrew Christians literally crucified Christ. The expression is a metaphor that places them in the company of those who had crucified Christ. Their life-style was little better.

● 7-8   In verses 7 and 8 the writer used, by analogy, the figure of land that had been abundantly watered and showed how one portion was fruitful and the other unfruitful. The former is a source of blessing while the latter, producing only "thorns and thistles," is rejected for burning. In like manner the works of some of the Hebrew Christians would be consigned to burning (but not themselves) "and near a curse" (v. 8).

● 9-12   The writer followed his discussion of the perils of apostasy (vv. 4-8) with words that bring both hope and encouragement to the Hebrew Christian. God would remember their labors and their love which they manifested for His namesake in their past ministries to the saints and in their continuing ministries to them. Paul stood persuaded of that, and he wanted the Hebrew Christians to understand it. The "better things" of verse 9 stand in contrast to the things pictured in 6:4-8.

Moreover, while the writer was dissatisfied with the life-style of the Hebrew

Christians (5:11-14); they still had not turned their backs on Christ (6:4-8). And though some of them were still as babes (*nēpioi*—5:13) rather than adults (*teleioi*, 5:14) and others were "in peril of becoming so,"[10] he did not lose hope for them and continued his longing for each one "to show the same zeal unto the fullness of the hope up to the end" (v. 11). He wanted them to advance in their knowledge of Christ and in their pursuit of the goal of the high calling of God that is in Christ Jesus. He longed for them to become mature Christians— spiritual adults. To this end, he hoped that they would not become *lazy* and *sluggish* (dull of hearing) in spiritual matters but rather become "imitators of those who, through faith and patient endurance, inherit the promises" (v. 12). From the word *imitators (mimētai)* comes our word *mimic*.

● 13-15   Here the writer turned to the example of Abraham which establishes, as Brooke Foss Westcott believed, two things: "The certainty of the hope which rests on a promise of God, and the need of patience in order to receive its fulfillment."[11] When God called Abraham to leave his country on a pilgrimage to an unknown land, He promised to make of him "a great nation" and to bless him and make his name great and charged him, in return, to be a blessing: "I will bless them that bless thee, and him that curseth thee will I curse: and in thee shall all the families of the earth be blessed" (Gen. 12:1-3).

In Israel two witnesses were required to establish a promise. In the case of Abraham, God established His promise to him with an oath which made it doubly secure. Abraham's pilgrimage was long and painful, but he remained patient and eventually saw the fulfillment of God's promise. Though he was old and his wife Sarah was barren, twenty-five years after he had left Ur a son, Isaac, was born. In the advent of Jesus and His atoning ministry as high priest after the order of Melchizedek, the promise to Abraham found its ultimate fulfillment. Just as the law was but a stage in the fulfillment of God's promise, even so was the promise to Abraham which in turn was but another stage in the fulfillment of the promises pointing to the advent and kingly high priesthood of Jesus. And the followers of Christ by the same patience will experience the fulfillment of God's promises for them both during the earthly pilgrimage and the full reward at the last day.

● 16-18   Here the emphasis lies on the nature of the oath which, constituting an appeal to higher authority, silenced all human contradictions and brought home to all the certainty of the divine promise. And God's promise to Abraham, certified by his oath, brings assurance to the people of God today in the promise further certified by the incarnation of Jesus and by His unique priestly ministry typified by the ministry of Melchizedek.

God's counsel is immutable. God's will is unchangeable. Abraham realized this by God's oath. We as Christ's followers realize this through His incarnate ministry. And all of this serves to give strong assurance and encouragement "to hold fast to the hope that is set before us" (AT).

● 19-20   The anchor, for the ancient seafarer, was "the symbol of hope."[12] The anchor of the soul of the Christian lies in Jesus Christ who Himself entered "the inner *sanctuary* of the curtain" (v. 19) thereby opening a sure and certain passageway for every person into the very presence of God. Previously, only the high priest could enter the holy of holies which symbolized the very presence of God and lay behind the heavy curtain which only the high priest could part to enter—once a year. And upon entering, the high priest dared not tarry lest he should violate by his own presence the presence of the living God. In Christ, however, the veil was rent from top to bottom, and all persons have equal access to God. The poorest of the poor or the richest of the rich can enter into the presence of God on any day, or any hour, in the quest of rest for the soul. For Jesus, going before us *(prodromos)* as a scout, not only mapped out the way but provided for us "an anchor of the soul" that is "both firm and secure." For by His atoning death in our behalf, Jesus became forever our High Priest "according to the order of Melchizedek." Every believer may lay hold on and cling to Him (Jesus Christ) in whom is our soul's best anchor.

Notes

1. A. T. Robertson, *Word Pictures in the New Testament,* vol. 5 (Nashville, Tenn.: Sunday School Board, SBC, 1931), p. 373.

2. Philip E. Hughes, *A Commentary on the Epistle to the Hebrews* (Grand Rapids, Mich.: William B. Eerdmans Publishing Company, 1977), p. 197.

3. Robertson, p. 374.

4. Herschel H. Hobbs, *Studies in Hebrews* (Nashville, Tenn.: Sunday School Board, SBC, 1954), p. 56.

5. R. Paul Caudill, *Philippians: A Translation with Notes* (Boone, N.C.: Blue Ridge Press of Boone, Inc., 1980), pp. 35-36.

6. Hobbs, p. 55 *ff.*

7. Joseph Henry Thayer. *A Greek-English Lexicon of the New Testament* (Grand Rapids, Mich.: Baker Book House. 1977), *in loco.*

8. Walter Bauer, *A Greek-English Lexicon of the New Testament* (Chicago: University of Chicago Press, 1979), *in loco*.

9. Robertson, p. 375.

10. Ibid., p. 377.

11. Brooke Foss Westcott, *The Epistle to the Hebrews: The Greek Text with Notes and Essays* (New York: MacMillan and Company, 1889), *in loco*.

12. William Barclay, *The Letter to the Hebrews* (Philadelphia: The Westminster Press, 1957), p. 63.

CHAPTER 7

Having previously introduced the Melchizedek priesthood of Christ, the writer now dealt with the matter in detail, finally proving that Christ as high priest after the order of Melchizedek, is superior to the Levitical priests and as such is High Priest forever. The writer based his analogy on two passages of Scripture in the Old Testament, Psalm 110:4 and Genesis 14:18-20, where suddenly this Melchizedek invaded the plane of history and as suddenly left. Melchizedek met Abraham in the King's Vale as he returned from the slaughter of the kings, gave him bread and wine, blessed him, and received tithes from Abraham. After this, Melchizedek disappeared, leaving behind only the two above-mentioned accounts of his ministry in the Old Testament. But in these sparse references, the writer to the Hebrews showed how Christ, as High Priest, foreshadowed by Melchizedek, is superior to the older Levitical type.

● 1-3   Here the writer presented a brief description of Melchizedek: (1) He was king of Salem. (2) He was priest "of God Most High." (3) He met Abraham in the King's Vale and blessed him as he returned from the slaughter of the kings. (4) He received tithes from Abraham. (5) His name by interpretation is King of righteousness. (6) He was also King of peace. (7) He was without genealogy—without father, without mother, and has no recorded beginning nor end of days. (8) He was made like unto the Son of God. (9) He abides as a priest forever. As priest "of God Most High," Melchizedek not only antedates the line of Aaron by hundreds of years but also represents "God's original priesthood."[1] The king of Sodom also met Abraham in the vale, along with Melchizedek. The kings whom Abraham slaughtered were: Amraphel, Arioch, Chedorlaomer, and Tidal. It was the custom of the victor to give a tithe of his spoils to the pagan gods.[2] The account in Genesis merely serves to point up the

125

analogy existing between Melchizedek and Christ, the chief difference being the fact that Jesus "continues priest in fact in heaven."[3]

● 4-10   Here the writer, having sketched the historical character of Melchizedek, now discussed his priesthood with reference to the priesthood of the Law. The contrast is clear. Note that by his name, Melchizedek was "King of righteousness" and also "King of peace." As Barclay noted, the order is "significant and inevitable." Before there can be peace, there must be righteousness (Rom. 5:1).

The law of the tithes decreed that the Levites who received no land were to receive a tithe of everything because of their priestly service in the tabernacle. But note that while the Levites received tithes from the people, Melchizedek received the tithe from Abraham which, by the reasoning of the Hebrews, meant that even the Levites themselves, through Abraham, paid tithes to Melchizedek. Abraham was the father of Isaac, Isaac the father of Jacob, and Jacob the father of Levi; therefore, by the Hebrew reckoning, Levi was still in the loins of Abraham when he paid tithes to Melchizedek. "This is a rabbinical imaginative refinement appealing to Jews."[4] Now Melchizedek, to whom Abraham paid tithes, was not of the Levitical line and is presented without genealogy whereas anyone who served as high priest, according to the Levitical law, had to be of the direct line of Levi, and the wife of the high priest had to be an Israelite. What is more, Melchizedek blessed Abraham, and by the same reckoning, the lesser is blessed by the greater.

While there is no record in Genesis of the death of Melchizedek, *there is one* "of whom it is witnessed that he liveth"—in vivid contrast to the priest of the Levites who are mortal and therefore dying men (v. 8). Melchizedek then was superior not only to Abraham but also to the Levitical priests in general. These Levitical priests who from generation to generation served as high priests were known to die. Therefore in their order there was "not only the contingency but the fact of succession."[5] Of course Abraham was not a priest, for the priesthood had not yet been instituted; but he did include "in himself, as the depositary of the divine promise and the divine blessing, all the forms, as yet undifferenti-ated, in which they were to be embodied."[6] Melchizedek then was a type of priesthood "independent of descent and uninterrupted by death."[7]

● 11-14   Here the translation is made from the imperfect (transitory) priesthood to the new (eternal) priesthood. Westcott briefly summarized Christ's priesthood that is after the order of Melchizedek: (1) new, (2) effective, (3) sure, (4) one. The argument, in a word, rests like this: if Melchizedek were a greater high priest than Levi, then Christ was superior both to Melchizedek and Levi, for Melchizedek was only a type, a shadow of the high priesthood that was to be in Christ and certainly superior to the priesthood of the Levites. After all, the Levitical priesthood, like the law, was transitional and transitory. The law was merely a schoolmaster addressing itself unto the people in their quest for spiritual maturity. Now if the Levitical priesthood had been adequate (on which basis the people received the law), what further need was there for "another priest to arise" according to the order of Melchizedek rather than according to the order of Aaron? And if there were the need of a more adequate high priest, there must of necessity be a change of the law, for the new and superior high priest came not from the tribe of Levi, as the law prescribed, but from Judah—Jesus sprang from the tribe of Judah, "with reference to which tribe Moses said nothing about priests" (v. 14).

● 15-19   Being transitory, the Levitical priesthood "was stamped with the conditions of limitation" during its continuance.[8] That it (the Levitical priesthood) was inadequate is clearly shown from the fact that the promise of another priesthood came while the Levitical priesthood was "still in full activity" (vv. 11-14).[9] What is more, this new high priesthood was spiritual, not legal, nor "sacerdotal only, but royal, not transitory but eternal."[10] Moreover, the old (Levitical) priesthood operated according to "the law of a carnal commandment" (vv. 16) whereas the new priesthood operated "according to the power of an indissoluble life" (vv. 16-17). Experience had shown that the law "made nothing perfect," and was by its very character transitory. Moreover, because of its "weakness and uselessness" (v. 18) there had to take place the annulment of the preceding commandment. In a word, there had to be "a better hope" (v. 19), a hope that made it possible for all people, however diverse their abilities and their character might be, to "come near to God" (v. 19).

● 20-22   Here the writer emphasized the fact that God with an oath instituted the new priesthood, the priesthood of Jesus, according to the order of Melchizedek whereas the Levitical priesthood was not so instituted. Those who served as priests in the Levitical system were mortal, appointed by law, and passed away. Not so of the priesthood of Jesus, for He is declared a priest by God with an oath, "and He will not change His mind, thou *art* a priest for ever" (v. 21).

By so much Jesus became a guarantee of "a better covenant." What is a covenant, and why was this covenant better? A covenant is simply an agreement between two parties whereby the faithful performance on the part of one party of the covenant enjoys a given response on the part of the other member of the covenant. In the case of the covenant between God and Israel, Israel was called upon to faithfully obey God's laws. God in return for faithful obedience granted Israel access to His presence. His covenant relationship is set forth in Exodus 24:1-8 where the people, in response to Moses' reading of the law said, "All that Jehovah hath spoken will we do, and be obedient" (Ex. 24:7). When there were acts of disobedience, the covenant relationship was broken, and the priest had to make sacrifices to restore the relationship. With Jesus, the covenant relationship is based upon love and His sacrifice of self. Under the new covenant mankind's access to God is not dependent upon his keeping a set of rules, but rather upon the redemptive love of God in Christ. And Jesus Christ Himself is the guarantee (surety) of this better covenant.

● 23-25   Many in number were those who had been "made priests" in the Levitical order for the simple reason that they were "being prevented by death from continuing" (v. 23). Not so of Jesus, for He holds the priesthood "permanently" (v. 24). This is why He is able to save "for all time those coming through Him to God" (v. 25), for He is *always living* "to make intercession for them." Jesus is not mortal as other priests. He lives forever, and is appointed by God to serve eternally as priest (v. 21) and God "will not change His mind" (AT).

● 26-28   Moreover, Jesus was a "fitting" High Priest for us, the writer said, because He is "holy, guileless, undefiled, separated from the sinners, and having become higher than the heavens." The word translated *holy (hosios)* is a word that signifies "the greatest of all goodnesses, the goodness which is pure in the sight of God."[11] "Having become higher than the heavens" (v. 26) probably harks back to the exaltation of Jesus and His ascension. In His personal life, Jesus was completely set apart unto the Father's will and sinless in all His ways—one "who did no sin" (1 Pet. 2:22). Moreover, in His relationship with others He was completely "guileless"; and, notwithstanding the sinful world in which He lived and the wiles of Satan, He remained "undefiled." For this reason, He was different from the high priests of the Levitical line. Before they could offer up sacrifices for the people, they had to offer up sacrifices for their own sins. But Jesus did no sin and made only one offering for the people, the offering of Himself as the Lamb of God, once and for all. The high priests, appointed according to the law, were men "having weakness" (v. 28); but Jesus, appointed by the word of the oath of God, was appointed "a Son made perfect forever," and of His office as High Priest, there can be no end. Moreover, being the character of person He was—in relationship to persons, to the sinful world about Him, and to God the Father—He was all the more superior to all other priests, and none other could ever be like Him.

Notes

1. Herschel H. Hobbs, *Studies in Hebrews* (Nashville, Tenn.: Sunday School Board, SBC, 1954), p. 60.
2. A. T. Robertson, *Word Pictures in the New Testament,* vol. 5 (Nashville, Tenn.: Sunday School Board, SBC, 1931), p. 380.
3. Ibid., p. 381.
4. Ibid., p. 383.
5. Brooke Foss Westcott, *The Epistle to the Hebrews: The Greek Text with Notes and Essays* (New York: MacMillan and Company, 1889), p. 180.
6. Ibid., p. 180.
7. Ibid., p. 181.
8. Ibid., p. 185.
9. Ibid.
10. Ibid.
11. William Barclay, *The Letter to the Hebrews* (Philadelphia: The Westminster Press, 1957), p. 89.

CHAPTER 8

Having described the holy, God-confirmed, eternal high priesthood of Christ, according to the order of Melchizedek, the writer next dealt with the manner in which the new High Priest carries on the duties of His office and the necessity for the nullification of the Levitical priesthood.

- 1-2   Here the writer called attention to the general character of Christ's high-priestly work. His position is that of royalty, for He has sat down "on the right hand of the throne of the majesty in the heavens." He is, therefore, both King and Priest. The words *throne of the Majesty* reflect the glory of His office over that of the old Mosaic priesthood. In this dual role as King and Priest, Christ serves as "a minister" of "the real Tent (tabernacle)" and of the holy places. His tent (tabernacle) was not pitched by individuals but was set up by the Lord, and its purpose was to serve the people and offer them direct access to the fellowship of God. And in His kingly role, He came "not to be ministered unto, but to minister, and to give his life a ransom for many" (Matt. 20:28). No high priest of the Levitical line could claim this position of honor and trust and service. They, appointed by men according to the law, came and went as the leaves of the forest; He came to serve forever, and death could never affect Him.

- 3-4   Since, by analogy, the priests of the Mosaic ritual were appointed "for the offering of both gifts and sacrifices," it was necessary for Christ, as High Priest, also to have "something that He may offer" (v. 3); and for that matter, were His priesthood on earth like that of the Levitical line, there would be no occasion for His service since there were those on earth who, according to the Mosaic ritual already were offering gifts "according to the law" (v. 4). Being of the tribe of Judah, rather than of Levi and being of divine appointment rather than by human appointment, "not at all would He be a priest."

● 5   After all, the priests of the Levitical line served only as "a model and shadow" (v. 5) of the heavenly things. This was made abundantly clear by God's warning to Moses concerning the tent (tabernacle) which he pitched in the wilderness. Every aspect of the tabernacle had to be according to the pattern (Ex. 25:40). See the words of Stephen (Acts 7:44).

● 6   "But now," that is with Jesus as the new High Priest in heaven, "He has attained a more excellent ministry" for two reasons: (1) He is mediator of a better covenant, and (2) the covenant has been "enacted upon better promises." The word *better (kreissōn)* is "the keynote of the Epistle."[1] Everything about Christianity is better: Jesus as High Priest (8:1-6); the sanctuary (8:2,5); the sacrifice (8:3 *ff.*); the Mediator (8:6); the covenant (8:6); the promises (8:6); the ministry itself as a whole (8:6).

● 7-13   Here the writer discussed at length this new covenant in its relationship to the covenant of the Levitical system which was transitory, imperfect, and but a shadowy outline of the new covenant that was to be.

The reason for the new covenant lay in the imperfection of the old covenant—that of the Levitical order. There the priests were mortal men. They died, and their office had to be filled repeatedly by other mortal men appointed according to the Levitical law. Moreover, those mortal priests had their imperfections—their sins which had to be atoned for. On the one day of the year when the high priest entered the holy of holies, therefore, his first deed was to offer a sacrifice for his own sins, for then, and then only, was he in position to offer a sacrifice for the sins of the people.

Christ as high priest offered for Himself no sacrifice because He had no sins. Having been tempted in all points as human beings, He still was without sin. And He made no repeated offerings, but a single offering consisting of Himself for the sins of the people of all time who would look to Him for forgiveness by faith. The Levitical priests were merely a "shadow" of His royal, priestly role.

Because of the imperfections of the Levitical priesthood, there was both a "moral and logical necessity" for a better priesthood,[2] and this was obtained by Jesus, who in turn became the "mediator of a better covenant" that rested on "better promises." The word *mediator (mesitēs)*, from an old word *mesos* (amid), meant "a middle man" or arbitrator.[3]

In discussing the first covenant and its shadowy character which anticipated something better that was to come, the writer quoted from the prophet

Jeremiah (31:31-34) in support of his premise concerning the superiority of the priesthood of Christ over that of the Mosaic ritual. Throughout the passage, the quotation deals with the covenant idea and its development in relationship to Israel. The word *covenant* (Greek *diathēke*) comes from an old compound word (*diatithēmi*) meaning "to put between" and stands for an agreement between two persons. The agreement is based on a mutual point of view whereby the agreement becomes void if either party violates the terms of the covenant. The word is familiar as a biblical idea, being used of the league entered into by Joshua and the Gibeonites (Josh. 9:6) and of the covenant between David and Jonathan (1 Sam. 23:18). The distinctive use in the Old Testament, however, relates to the covenant relationship between God and Israel.[4] (See Deut. 4:23.) There is another Greek word used for an agreement between persons, or bond, or covenant, and that word is *sunthēke*. But the word *sunthēke* is used of agreements wherein the participants who enter into the agreement are on an equality. Each participant "can bargain with the other and propose terms to the other."[5] This is not true of the covenant between God and Israel, or God and humanity. They do not meet "on equal terms." In this relationship, "the whole offer comes from God. It is God who comes to man and who offers this relationship with Himself and who states the terms on which this relationship will remain effective."[6] No bargaining on the part of humanity with God! God makes the offer, and humanity is free to reject or accept it, but we are not free to alter it. This is why the word used for the covenant (*diathēke*) in the New Testament is used for *a will*. In a *will* the testator makes it. The other party can accept it if he or she desires or reject it, but cannot alter it. So it is of our relationship with God. If we accept God's covenant, we must do so on God's terms. We cannot in any way alter the terms. What is more, according to God's ancient covenant with Israel, the covenant was valid only so long as the people who accepted the covenant kept it (Ex. 24:1-8). Herein lies the necessity for a new kind of covenant. Humanity was not able to keep the old covenant in all of its points, for human beings did not have the moral and spiritual strength necessary to do so.

That the first covenant failed to achieve its purpose with the people of Israel is obvious from the fact that all of those above twenty years of age failed to reach the Promised Land. They died in the wilderness. The reason for their death was their covenant breaking. There was nothing wrong with the covenant that God made with them. It would have been effective had they lived up to it. They were still God's people. They did not lose their redemption from Egypt. They never again went back under the bondage of Pharaoh. But they failed to reach the goal God had for them in the Promised Land. Only their young were privileged to achieve that destiny along with Joshua and Caleb. Moses himself was excluded from that stage of achievement. So there had to be another covenant— a new covenant, for if the first covenant had been "faultless," there would have been no need for a second.

Now in Greek (the language in which the New Testament was originally written) there are two words for new: (1) *neos* which means "new" as to *time*. In the assembly line of an automobile factory, each automobile that rolls off the assembly line is "new" in point of time. But this does not mean that the quality of it is different, or the kind of it is different. (2) The word used for this *new covenant* is the word *kainos* which means "new" not only with reference to time but also in *quality*. The writer further described the quality of the old covenant made with the fathers of the Israelites as "becoming obsolete and growing old" and "near disappearance" (v. 13). But there is another difference that marks the New Covenant. It is a covenant of the mind and of the heart: "Putting my laws into their mind,/And upon their hearts I will write them" (v. 10). This New Covenant is not of law but of grace, and it is to be written "in their intellect or moral understanding."[7] This New Covenant is to unify the house of Judah and that of Israel which had split into two kingdoms, leaving Judah with two tribes and Israel with ten, 1,000 years before. The schism was to be done with. Old enmities would cease. This New Covenant, to be written in the hearts of persons, would bring about a new relationship of loving fellowship both between humanity and God and among persons themselves. The relationship was to be personal, a relationship that springs from love rather than from fear. But obedience comes not from the ordered fulfillment of the law, but from the deep desire of loving hearts to know and to do God's will.

"The most tremendous thing about the new covenant was that it made man's relationship to God no longer dependent on man's obedience. It became entirely dependent on God's love."[8] Humanity is still under a responsibility but not the responsibility that comes from the observance of a multitude of laws which, under the multiplying hands of the scribes, became a virtual impossibility to keep; and this New Covenant is to be available to all "from the small to the great" (v. 11). Each will share the same mercy of God. Each will know the same forgiveness of sin as each looks to God by faith. For God's promise (v. 12) is to be "merciful *in relation* to their iniquities," and as to their sins He promises to "remember no more."

One further thing remains to be said with reference to the old and the new covenants: "In the saying 'new' *(covenant)*, He has treated the first *covenant* as obsolete; and "that which is becoming obsolete and growing old is near disappearance" (v. 13).

Notes

1. A. T. Robertson, *Word Pictures in the New Testament,* vol. 5 (Nashville, Tenn.: Sunday School Board, SBC, 1931), p. 391.
2. Ibid., p. 389.
3. Ibid., p. 391.
4. William Barclay, *The Letter to the Hebrews* (Philadelphia: The Westminster Press, 1957), p. 98.
5. Ibid.
6. Ibid.
7. Herschel H. Hobbs, *Studies in Hebrews* (Nashville, Tenn.: Sunday School Board, SBC, 1954), p. 75.
8. Barclay, p. 102.

CHAPTER 9

Having introduced the character of the new covenant by quoting at length from the prophet Jeremiah (31:31-34), the writer turned to the first covenant and discussed the old sanctuary and its arrangements (vv. 1-10) before placing in gripping contrast the Levitical priesthood with the high-priestly ministry of Christ. Although the recipients of the epistle must have been entirely familiar with his words concerning the first tabernacle and its beautiful appointments, it is fitting that we call to mind, here, the lovely character of this first tabernacle that was but a shadowy representation of the heavenly tabernacle.

● 1-5   This first tabernacle was prepared because the first covenant had "regulations for worship and the earthly sanctuary" (v. 1, AT). A splendid description of the wilderness tabernacle is found in Exodus 25—31 and 35—40. The tabernacle (for a Hebrew word meaning "dwelling"—from another Hebrew word meaning "to dwell") was the portable sanctuary or sacred "tent" erected by Moses at God's command. It represented the meeting place of the God of Israel with His people. In the tabernacle was the ark that accompanied Israel while they were in the wilderness. Upon reaching the Promised Land, the ark was located for a while at a number of different places in Canaan but was finally replaced by Solomon's Temple. This portable place of worship accompanied the people all the way from Sinai to Jerusalem. Referred to variously by the word *sanctuary,* the "Tent of Meeting" (Ex. 33:7; Num. 11:16; etc.), the word is usually rendered in the Greek of the Bible by the words *he skēnē tou marturiou* which means "the tent of the testimony." The heavenly tabernacle was not the work of the hands of men, for it is of the invisible order, an order in which human hands find no channel of expression. And this heavenly tabernacle with all of its meaning was accomplished through Christ's passion and His resurrection and found the fullness of satisfaction in the glorious triumph of the ascension. God enjoined Moses to make Him a sanctuary that He might dwell among them (Ex. 25:8), and when the Israelites were made aware of God's purpose by Moses, they gave generously that such a tabernacle might be built. The tabernacle of course consisted of a tent that was constructed and pitched according to God's orders. It was a tent by necessity, for the people were dwelling in tents in the wilderness as they journeyed on their pilgrimage toward the Promised Land. The chief purposes of the transitory tabernacle were two: "It was designed on the one hand to symbolise the Presence of God among His people; and on the other to afford under such restrictions a means of approach to Him."[1] But the fact that there were "restrictions" meant that access to God's presence was not yet fully realized.

The tabernacle which symbolized God's presence among His people was divided into two parts called the *holy place* and the *holy of holies*. The complete description of the tabernacle occurs in Exodus (25—31 and 35—40). In the first tent (v. 2), called the holy place, there was the golden lampstand on the south side while on the north side were the table and the loaves of presentation. Twelve cakes made up the showbread, and they were replaced each week by the priests who were permitted to eat of the showbread which symbolized the divine Presence. Then there was the altar of incense where incense was burned each morning and evening "symbolising the prayers of the people rising to God."[2] Behind the second curtain (vv. 3-5) was the tent called the holy of holies. Within this area rested the ark of the covenant "covered on all sides with gold" and in which were (1) a golden jar holding the manna, (2) the rod (of Aaron that sprouted), (3) the two tables of stone on which were written God's covenant with His people (Ex. 24:12; 25:16). Resting upon the lid of the ark were the golden cherubim of glory with their outstretched wings "overshadowing the mercy-seat." It was at this point that the presence of God was symbolized: "I will commune with thee from above the mercy-seat, from between the two cherubim which are upon the ark of the testimony" (Ex. 25:22). The priest entered the first tabernacle from day to day performing the rituals (v. 6), but into the second tabernacle the high priest alone would go, once a year, and "not without blood," which he offered first for himself and then for the sins of the people (v. 7).

● 6-7   Burnt offerings were offered from day to day by the priests in the *first tabernacle* (v. 6), but there were also other stated occasions for the offering of sacrifices by the priests as ordered in Numbers 28—29: continual burnt offerings (28:3) and offerings on the sabbath (28:9), the new year (28:11), the Passover (28:16), the day of the first-fruits (28:26), and the feast of the trumpets (29:1). There were also offerings in addition to those at the appointed feasts—votive offerings, freewill offerings, burnt offerings, drink offerings, peace offerings (Num. 29:39), etc.

But while the priests entered the first tabernacle continually performing the prescribed rituals, only the high priest could enter the second tabernacle, the holy of holies, and that but once during the year. There he could only enter with blood which he in turn offered first for himself, then for the sins of the people (v. 7). The fact that even the priests and high priests were limited in their approach to God indicated that while the way of the law was "symbolic and disciplinary," it was but a shadowy outline of the perfect system that was to follow.[3] The old order was obviously "preparatory" and for the present season which was to give way to the coming of the perfect order in Christ. It is significant, however, that in the old order the high priest gained the entrance into God's presence through blood whereas Christ by His own blood made the redemptive offering.

Erected out of voluntary gifts on the part of the people, a list of the materials is found in Exodus 25:3 *ff.* In the outer shrine called the holy place, and separated from the holy of holies by a curtain, was the table of the showbread on the north side. On the south side stood the seven-branched golden lampstand while, according to Exodus 30:1-5, the altar of incense stood in front of the veil which separated the holy place from the holy of holies.

In the construction of the tabernacle, there seemed to be a sort of graduated holiness which allowed the people to come as far as the court while the priests only could enter the holy place; only the high priest could enter the holy of holies on the Day of Atonement, and this was to be done "throughout your generations" (Ex. 30:10).

Before entering the holy of holies, on the Day of Atonement, the high priest washed himself, dressed in fine linen garments, and taking the blood of a bullock, parted the curtain, and entered the holy of holies. The ritual was elaborate involving the creation of a cloud by placing incense in the foyer so that the mercy-seat would be hidden from his view lest he die. After making atonement for his own sins the high priest made atonement for the sins of his people, sprinkling the mercy-seat with the blood of the sacrificial goat as done with the blood of the bullock. Thus with the blood of both the bullock and the goat, the holy place was cleansed as well as the tabernacle of the congregation. The scapegoat, chosen by lot, was let loose into the wilderness to die, carrying with it, symbolically, the sins of the people.

Following the ritual in the holy of holies the priest reentered the tabernacle of the congregation, removed his garments, and bathed again, dressed in his other garments, and offered again burnt offerings both for himself and for the people.

● 8-10   Here the writer went on to point out that the ministry of the wilderness sanctuary, and all the Mosaic rituals pertaining to the sanctuary, were to be considered merely as "a figure for the time present" in which both the sacrifices and gifts that were made were "unable in relation to the conscience to make perfect the one worshiping" (v. 9, AT). After all, the Holy Spirit made it abundantly clear that "the way into the Holy Place has not yet been made manifest, while the first tabernacle is still standing" (v. 8, AT). What is more, the "different washings," "meats and drinks," and other regulations pertaining to the body held only "until the time of the new order" (v. 10, AT). But now with the advent of Christ, there is a new High Priest "of good things realized already" (v. 11) for now there is "the greater and more perfect tabernacle, not made with hands—that is, not of this creation" (v. 11, AT). After all, the fact that only the high priest could enter the holy of holies which symbolized the actual access to God's presence, and that but once a year, was sufficient to indicate that the true access to God's presence had not yet been made available to all the people. The hopes, the dreams, the expectations of the people were there as they had been through the years; but the imperfections were likewise still manifest so long as the old order was in force. When Christ died on Calvary as the Lamb of God for the sins of the world, the old order was completely superseded. It had become obsolete, near vanishing. And this was accomplished "not through the blood of goats and calves, but through His own blood" (v. 12, AT), for in entering the holy place, Christ entered "once for all" having already obtained "eternal redemption" for all who would come through Him by faith to God. In Christ, however, the full realization did come; for through His own blood, Christ "through the eternal Spirit offered Himself without blemish to God" (v. 14, AT), and thereby He made possible the cleansing of the conscience "from dead works to serve the living God" (v. 14).

● **11-14** The redemption which Christ obtained is eternal (v. 12) whereas the redemption offered by the Mosaic ritual was a limited, recurring thing. Even the annual atoning act of redemption had to be repeated each year, and that on the same date.

The heavenly tabernacle then was entirely different, and of a new order. As ancient scholars held: "This new tabernacle which brought men into the very presence of God was nothing else than the body of Jesus. He came here in a body, in a tabernacle. And by so coming He brought God to men and He brought men into the presence of God."[4] And the superiority of the priesthood of Christ lies in the soul-cleansing of Christ's sacrifice—cleansing that is eternal in its redemptive nature—a redemption that took them out from under the dominion of sin forever giving the worshiper the power to achieve a new life-style and the ability "to serve the living God" (v. 14). To follow the reasoning of Westcott, Jesus in sacrificing Himself made the superior sacrifice because His sacrifice was *voluntary, spontaneous, rational,* and *moral.*[5] There was nothing mechanical about His sacrifice, nothing of legalism, for it was brought about by means of *the eternal spirit.*

● **15-22** Because of His atoning sacrifice (vv. 12-14), the writer said that Christ is "the mediator of a new covenant," a covenant that does not call for continuing acts of sacrifice, blood, and otherwise as was true of the Levitical ritual but rather for a sacrifice that is eternal, and that does not depend upon the mechanical administrations of men according to set laws. "The real value," said Robertson, "in the typical sacrifices under the Old Testament system was in the realization in the death of Christ. It is Christ's death that gives worth to the types that pointed to him."[6] Actually, as Robertson went on to point out, Christ's atoning sacrifice "is the basis of the salvation of all who are saved before the Cross and since."[7] That is the why of the symbols and rites of the old Levitical order. They were all bound up in God's purpose for the redemption of the world.

In verses 15 and 16, the word *diathēkē* is used in a double sense. In verse 15 it is translated "covenant," whereas in verse 16 it is rendered "testament." The use of the word in verse 16 conveys the sense of "a will" or "testament." Now the testament (will) can be operative (effective) only following the death of the testator ("the death of him who made it must be made publicly known,"

v. 16, AT). In other words, the will becomes valid only when the person who made the will dies. It is never operative while the one who made it is still living (v. 17). The writer went on to support his statement with the fact that "even the first *covenant*" was not dedicated "without blood" (v. 18) and illustrated his premise by the action of Moses who, upon communicating the commandments of the laws of God to the people, took "the blood of the calves [and of the goats], with water and red wool and hyssop," and "sprinkled both the book itself and all the people" (v. 19, AT). It was customary to mix water with the blood and sprinkle it by use of a wisp of wool or a stem of hyssop (Num. 19:6). The writer made no mention of the use of oil as is done in Exodus 40:9 *ff.* and Leviticus 8:10 *ff.* It is also interesting to note that in Exodus the author did not mention the sprinkling of the book of the covenant as does the writer in the Epistle to the Hebrews (v. 19). He did indicate the sprinkling of the tabernacle and all of the vessels used in priestly services "likewise with the blood" (v. 21, AT), for this use of "the blood of the covenant" (v. 20) was in accord with God's command for a lost world.

In the Levitical sacrificial system (Lev. 17:11) are the words: "For the life of the flesh is in the blood; and I have given it to you upon the altar to make atonement for your souls: for it is the blood that maketh atonement, by reason of the life." This harks back to the beginning of the covenant relationship between God and Israel. When Moses took the book of the covenant and read it "in the audience of the people" they said, "All that Jehovah hath spoken will we do, and be obedient" (Ex. 24:7). Having already thrown half of the blood offering against the altar, Moses then took the blood he had put in the basins and threw it upon the people saying, "Behold the blood of the covenant which Jehovah hath made with you concerning all these words" (Ex. 24:8). Here emerges the basic Hebrew principle in the Hebrew sacrificial system, namely, that without the shedding of blood there can be no cleansing, no purifying, or ratification of the covenant with God. Without such, "there is no forgiveness of sin" (v. 22, AT). The words *and almost everything is cleansed with blood* (v. 22) implies that there were exceptions. (See Lev. 5:11 *ff.*)

● 23-28   This is why it was necessary for Christ to shed His own blood on Calvary. For the New Covenant to be inaugurated as an atoning act for the forgiveness of sin, Christ had to enter, once and for all, into the sacrificial act as Lamb of God for the sins of the world.

The reasoning is that since it was necessary under the old covenant for blood sacrifices to be made in behalf of forgiveness of sins and since "the copies of the things in the heavens" (v. 23) could only be cleansed in this way, it was all the more necessary for the heavenly things to employ "better sacrifices than these" (v. 23).

Any difficulty experienced in verse 24 portraying the entrance of Christ "into heaven itself," now to appear before the face of God in our behalf is simply an extension of the comparison between the shadow and the real (see Ex. 24—25). At every point in the analogy, Christ fulfilled the high priestly role as it was foreshadowed in the Mosaic ritual. Just as the High Priest entered the holy of holies on the Day of Atonement bearing blood, Christ appeared in heaven by means of His own sacrifice *once for all,* thereby giving humanity eternal access to God. Christ's appearance was a face-to-face matter. He approached him on the "eye level," a reference which harks back to the Oriental custom of kings in relation to the "seating [of] dignitaries of equal rank so that when they looked at one another, their faces or eyes met on an even line."[8]

After all, the Holy Place entered by Christ was not made with hands of men as was that of the Levitical order which was only "a copy of the true" (v. 24, AT), So into heaven itself entered Christ "now to appear before the face of God in our behalf" (v. 24). And this He did "once for all," and not "frequently" as the high priests did who entered into the holy place annually, bringing blood "not his own" (v. 25) for the cleansing of the sins of themselves and the people. Otherwise, Christ's high-priestly role would have called for Him "to suffer often, from the foundation of the world" (v. 26, AT). But in Him there was consummation of the copy image which characterized the cleansing role by the priest under the old covenant. With the consummation "of the ages," therefore, Christ manifested Himself as man's mediator and the instrument of the removal of His sin "through the sacrifice of Himself" (v. 26, AT). This He did "once for all," and not to be repeated as was necessary on the part of the priests of the Levitical order. In Him, there would be no more an annual day of atonement, for the atonement He made was eternal and bears no need for repetition.

"Before the foundation of the world," that is, Christ's sacrifice is final and absolute, leaving no need or opportunity for anyone to follow in His train (1 Pet. 1:19 *ff.*; Rev. 13:8). The words *for the removal of the sin* in verse 26 refer to "sin as a principle" whereas in the Levitical order the sacrifice was for "individual transgressions."[9] For since Christ's sacrifice had to do with "sin as a principle," it is obvious that the efficacy of that sacrifice "reaches through all time past and future" for those who look to God by faith.[10]

In verses 27 and 28 there is an unusual parallelism by analogy in which the writer said: "Just as it is laid up for men once to die, and after this the judgment, so also the Christ, having been offered once to bear the sins of many, shall appear a second time, without relation to sin, to them that eagerly await Him unto salvation" (vv. 27-28, AT). The words *after this the judgment* recall the words of Jesus who reminded His followers that they would meet Christ as Judge (Matt. 25:31-46; John 5:25-29). "Death lies stored in the future, 'laid up' for each man."[11]

Verse 28 offers glorious assurance of the ultimate return of Christ (the second coming), and "without relation to sin," for there is no hint of "a second chance" at that time. At Christ's second coming the burden that He took upon Himself concerning the sins of humanity on the occasion of His first manifestation will not exist since His sacrifice has already been made. The words *unto salvation* refer to the final stage of salvation, the stage that is to be realized at the last day in heaven. Those who have been saved, and who day by day are engaged in "working out" their own salvation (that is, progressing in their day-to-day growth and development toward the final realization of the redemptive purpose of God in Christ Jesus) at the same time eagerly await His second coming that will usher in the Day of days!

Notes

1. Brooke Foss Westcott, *The Epistle to the Hebrews: The Greek Text with Notes and Essays* (New York: MacMillan and Company, 1889), p. 258.
2. William Barclay, *The Letter to the Hebrews* (Philadelphia: The Westminster Press, 1957), p. 105.
3. Westcott, p. 251.
4. Barclay, p. 113.
5. Ibid., p. 115 *ff*.
6. A. T. Robertson, *Word Pictures in the New Testament,* vol. 5 (Nashville, Tenn.: Sunday School Board, SBC, 1931), p. 400 *ff*.
7. Ibid.
8. Herschel H. Hobbs, *Studies in Hebrews* (Nashville, Tenn.: Sunday School Board, SPC, 1954), p. 99.
9. Robertson, p. 404.
10. Westcott, p. 276.
11. Ibid., p. 278.

CHAPTER 10

The writer of the epistle graphically portrayed in the preceding section the sharp contrast between the complete high-priestly work of Christ and that of the repetitious, annual priestly offerings of the Levitical high priest. The work of Christ as High Priest was accomplished in one complete, single act of sacrifice on the cross—never to be repeated by another. The offerings of the Levitical high-priest were continual, year by year. The Day of Atonement was meaningful only for one year, for it had to be repeated, annually. So it was of all the Levitical sacrifices. They were imperfect, and temporary, whereas the sacrifice of Christ's high-priestly work was complete and final. The argument that follows supports what has gone before dealing in a general way with the Levitical sacrifices.

● 1-3   Here the writer made clear that the Levitical sacrifices were powerless, though offered year by year, to deliver humanity from its sinful consciousness. In the first place, these sacrifices were only *shadows* of "the good things to come" and not even "the very image" of those good things. The word for shadow *(skian)* indicates "a pale, nebulous reflection, a mere outline or silhouette, a form without reality and without substance."[1] The word *image* indicates a representation that is more detailed—complete—as that of a portrait or photograph. These year-by-year sacrifices do not even offer a good picture of those good things which relate to the high-priestly work of Christ. What is more, these acts of sacrifice, which are no more than mere shadows of the real sacrifice that is to be, are powerless to make perfect "them that draw nigh."

Moreover, had these Levitical sacrifices been able to effect the cleansing of the worshipers, the worshipers would not have continued to have a "consciousness of sins" in the same measure. They would have realized that they had become members of the family of God, His children; moreover, they would have known that "if any man sin," being a child of the King, he would have "an Advocate with the Father, Jesus Christ the righteous" who is the "propitiation for our sins; and not for ours only, but also for the whole world" (1 John 2:1-2).

In the Levitical sacrifices there was the consciousness of inadequacy. Every year they had to go through the same ritual again. Every year, there had to be the Day of Atonement. Every year there was a reminder (v. 3) that the whole process of deliverance from sin had to be started all over again. The Day of Atonement and all the sacrifices and offerings that had taken place previously were not enough to assure the worshiper of complete justification.

● 4   Moreover, the worshipers were faced with a continuing impossibility, namely, that the blood of bulls and goats are not able to "take away sins." The repetition of the sacrifices, year by year, became the perfect rebuttal for the claims of the efficacy of the Levitical sacrifice, and the annual repetition of the sacrifices merely served "to keep alive the recollection of sin as a present burden."[2] After all, goats and bulls are both "unwilling and unconscious" sacrifices, and the very act of such is irrational, and with such humanity can have no lasting satisfaction.

● 5-10   Here again the writer depicted the sacrifice of Christ as the one and only valid sacrifice which in itself, once and for all, amounts to the perfect fulfillment of God's will. And this Christ accomplished through perfect obedience. Quoting from a messianic passage in Psalm 40 (6-8), the writer continued to emphasize the displeasure of God in sacrifices and offerings of the Levitical order in which the Messiah says, "I have come (in the roll of the book it is written of Me), To do, O God, Thy will" (v. 7, AT). The repetition of the animal-offering *(thusian)*, the burnt-offering *(holokautōmata)*, the meal-offering *(prosphoran)*, and the sin-offering *(peri hamartias)* brought no pleasure to God (v. 6). Because of this, the Messiah, referring to the prophetic reference of His forthcoming messiahhood, speaks, saying, "Lo, I am come/To do thy will." Herein, therefore, by His perfect obedience, He abolishes the priesthood ritual of the Mosaic order and establishes His own high-priestly role as Messiah. That which animal sacrifices could not do, Christ did perfectly in the sacrificial offering of His own body on the tree. " 'He came to be a great High Priest, and the body was prepared for him, that by the offering of it he might put sinful men for ever into the perfect religious relation to God' (Denney, *The Death of Christ*, p. 234)."[3] Christ's perfect obedience, in the sacrifice of His own body, made possible the sanctification of His followers (*hēgiasmenoi esmen*). The verb form is periphrastic perfect passive indicative of the old word *hagiazo*, meaning "to set apart unto the will of God, for His good pleasure, to *sanctify*." And the verb form means that this "setting apart," this "sanctification," took place in the past and still holds. It was not a process that had to be repeated each year as was true of the Levitical offerings. The salvation process, of course, did and does go on year by year with a view to the fullness of the realization of one's perfect salvation at the last day. But annual sacrifices are not required for this, for the one sacrifice of Christ on the cross was complete and final for all time.

● 11-14   Here we have a further portrayal of Christ's preeminence as High Priest and of the effective, abiding character of His sacrifice. The contrast between the priesthood of Christ and that of the Levitical order is strong and arresting. Whereas the Levitical priest stands daily (v. 11) offering the same sacrifices which have never been able to take away sins, Christ, on the other hand, offered but one sacrifice for sins; and that sacrifice could never be repeated, for His act was complete and final. Nothing was lacking. Moreover, He "sat down" at the right hand of God following His sacrifice, thereby assuming His position of royalty (vv. 12-13), whereas the Levitical priests continued to stand daily in ministering their offerings and sacrifices (v. 11). There was no need for them to sit down, for their work was of a continuing nature and without efficacy at that. Here we come to the main point of the contrast as Robertson noted: "The one sacrifice does the work that the many failed to do."[4] The words *from now on waiting expectantly"* reflect the confidence of Christ in final and certain victory (see John 16:33 and 1 Cor. 15:24-28). The *one* offering of Christ became efficacious forever for all those whose lives are "sanctified" (*hagiazomenous*, v. 14), that is, consecrated, dedicated. The word *hagiazomenous* is used extensively in the New Testament of those "whose lives are set apart for or unto God, to be exclusively his."[5] The participle is present passive, for the process is "still going on" in many persons (2:11).[6] The glorious aspect of the experience is that they are "perfected for ever" (v. 14). The process is progressive, for Christians continue to grow in wisdom and knowledge in proportion as they apply themselves to the study of God's Word, in daily efforts to translate into life His concepts of truth and duty. God saved the Israelites from the clutches of Pharaoh, but they failed to go on toward the fulfillment of God's promises for them. They failed to reach the stage of their development that would have put them in the Promised Land. God has a purpose, a plan, for every life. And the Christian is to advance in the day-by-day effort to realize the fulfillment of that purpose.

● 15-18   Here Christ is presented as the perfect fulfillment of the New Covenant previously described by the prophet Jeremiah (see 31:31 *ff.*). At the heart of the New Covenant fulfilled by Christ was the establishment of an effective and eternal means for the forgiveness of sins for all who come to Him in faith. In His sacrifice on the cross, once and for all, the Levitical sin offerings as previously practiced under the old order became no longer necessary, for the Mosaic ritual of sin offerings no longer had merit for believers. This basis of forgiveness of sin is attested to by the Holy Spirit (v. 15), for the laws of God are put upon the hearts and the minds of believers who, in this new principle, obtain direct access to God. Notice in verse 17 how the writer spoke of their *sins (hamartiōn)* and their *transgressions (anomiōn)*. Whatever the character of the sin, the believer finds forgiveness and refuge in Christ.

● 19-25   These verses present a resumé of the second of five arguments concerning the superiority of Christ's work as High Priest over that of the Levitical order. The first argument was presented in 8:1-6, and three others are to follow. Along with the premise is an earnest exhortation to the Hebrew Christians to "keep on holding fast the confession of our hope without wavering" (AT). Obviously, there were those who were tempted by Satan (even as Christ was tempted) to desert their Christian pilgrimage.

The holy place refers to the heavenly sanctuary into which Jesus, the forerunner, entered before us (6:18-20). This sanctuary is better than that of the Levitical order, for it was made possible by the sacrifice by Jesus of His own blood (v. 19). The way He opened for believers is *a new and living way through the curtain of his own flesh* (v. 20). There as the *great High Priest,* He presides at "the house of God" (v. 21). Note the parallelism in the picture: whereas in the Levitical order the Christian gained access into God's presence by means of the blood of bulls and goats, in the New Covenant the Christian himself enters the holy of holies in the blood of Christ; for in the new order every believer is ideally part of a kingdom of priests—the hope of Jehovah for the children of Israel as He brought them out of bondage. Christians, therefore, are to "keep on coming *to God* with a true heart in full assurance of faith" (v. 22, AT) for we have a mission to fulfill. We are on a pilgrimage that is to engage us every day of our lives, a pilgrimage that is to experience the ultimate fulfillment in heaven. God expects a response on the part of His people that is worthy of the redemption that has come to them, and of the promises that are laid away for them in heaven. There is to be no wavering in faith (v. 22-23).

What is more, the Hebrew Christians are expected to lend encouragement to one another in the matter of "love and good works" (v. 24); and one way that this can be done is for them not to forsake their own "assembling together" as was the habit with some people. There is no place for despair on the part of those who confess hope in the Lord Christ. The word *encouraging (paroxusmon)* furnishes us our word *paroxysm* meaning *to stimulate, to sharpen, to incite, stir up emotion,* and here in the good sense "unto love and good works." The words *not forsaking* mean, literally, "not leaving behind, not leaving in the lurch" (as in 2 Tim. 4:10). The tendency to drift into the habit of nonattendance at church is an old, old tendency, and it is much a problem today. This is obvious in the building of the church meeting place (the sanctuary) which almost invariably anticipates an attendance that is far smaller than the resident membership of the given church. In verse 22 the writer gave us a terse characterization of true worshipers: (1) a true heart, (2) fullness of faith, (3) pure hearts, (4) careful regard for the body, the temple of the holy Spirit. "The Day drawing near" obviously refers to the second coming of Christ, and the passing of every single day brings His return nearer (v. 25, AT).

● 26-31   Here the writer dealt boldly and realistically with the perils of backsliding (apostasy). The passage calls for comparison with 6:4-8, and reflects the same tragic consequences for those who, having been "enlightened and tasted of the heavenly gift, and were made partakers of the Holy Spirit," then failed to cooperate with God as did the Israelites in the wilderness, and thereby fall short of God's intended goal for them on the pilgrimage. Every believer who has been born of the Spirit has a personal responsibility that cannot, with impunity, be neglected. It is the same old story of being saved as by fire. For such persons sacrifice does not avail, just as was true of the Israelites in the wilderness. No matter if they had offered ten thousand sacrifices after God had spoken, the sacrifices would have been fruitless. They simply had lost their opportunity to enter the Promised Land. They had been *saved* from the impending doom under Pharaoh, but they lost their opportunity to proceed with Joshua and Caleb and the younger ones into the Land of Promise where they would spend the balance of their days on earth in joyful fellowship with God in the continuing fulfillment of His purpose for them and others. In verse 26 the idea is that of *deliberate* sins on the part of those who have received "the knowledge of the truth," and yet have gone on in their *backsliding*. All that is left for such is "a certain fearful expectation of judgment" (v. 27).

The judgment of God at the last day *is* a fearful thing to contemplate, but something that every person must face, and there is no partiality with God. To emphasize the severity of the judgment and of the consequences of failure to cooperate with God in His effort, through Christ, to redeem the lost world, the author harks back to the Old Testament whereby those who broke the covenant relationship (Deut. 17:1-7) through idolatrous worship could die at the mouth of two or three witnesses. By their life-styles, they lost their usefulness to their fellow believers. Arguing from the lesser to the greater, the writer compared the severity of the punishment under the New Covenant with the punishment of those who broke their covenant relationship under the old covenant. To emphasize all the more the gravity of standing off from the holy mission of worldwide redemption in which every believer is to share in Jesus Christ, the writer made clear his point with two quotations from Deuteronomy (32:35 and 32:36). The Lord God is living and active, and though His patience is boundless, there has to be—in the end—a judgment day. The wrath of God is as real as His love which He manifested in the incarnation of His Son. And this *wrath* "is revealed from heaven against all ungodliness and unrighteousness of men, who hinder the truth in unrighteousness" (Rom. 1:18).

What the writer had in mind here was not "particular" sins so much as the transgression of the covenant relationship that has its analogy with Israel who at Kadesh-barnea, by her willful sin of provocation, manifested her indifference as a nation to the fulfillment of her mission under God as a redeemed people. They were simply cut off from continuing as cosharers in God's redemptive purpose which would have taken them into the Land of Promise. Such conduct as that at Kadesh-barnea marked them as unfit participants in the furtherance of their growth and development as the people of God who were, by divine purpose, to serve as a generation of priests, a holy nation. The Israelites had experienced God's redemptive grace, for He had delivered them from Egypt; but they were guilty of "the sin of *standing off from* God (6:6) as he seeks to lead them on in Christian development for service."[8] All the sacrifices in the world would have been fruitless in an effort to restore the willfully disobedient Israelites to their share in the realization of the Promised Land experience. That was a stage in their intended growth and development that they could never attain.

● 32-34   Perhaps harking back to the words of Moses to Israel (Deut. 32:7), the writer issued a stirring challenge to the Hebrew Christians. They, too, had experienced "days of old" which they needed to recall. They, too, had seen persecution. They, too, had suffered reproach. They had known what it was to be "publicly exposed" (AT). They, too, had been "a gazing-stock" (v. 33). But having been "enlightened," they were able to endure the "hard struggle of sufferings" (v. 32, AT). Nevertheless, the Hebrew Christians had "sympathized with the prisoners" (v. 34, AT) and had "accepted the plundering" of their belongings joyfully, for they were confident that they had "a better possession and one that is permanent" (v. 34, AT). Moreover, they needed to continue to endure with patience and boldness their continuing conflicts so that "having done the will of God" they might yet receive the *promise*.

● 35-36   Robertson felt that the Jewish Christians in question "were in peril of a panic and of stampeding away from Christ."[9] For the believer, the line of demarcation is clearly and tightly drawn. Promises of God that relate to a bright and happy future in the development and exercise that belong to the faithful in Christ cannot be enjoyed by those who "stand off" and fail to follow in His train. If they have experienced regeneration and the *enlightenment* that comes with it, they will be saved at the last day though as "by fire." Their works will suffer the condemnation of God in the judgment. They had shown great boldness in the past. But there still remained the need for *boldness*, and that had its own *reward*. They must continue the pilgrimage in this same spirit of boldness, understanding, and devotion both to God and to their fellow Christians. In other words, if the person keeps up the sin habit, and does not turn to the Lord, after receiving the full knowledge of the truth, there is nothing else to do for the person (v. 26). By such an attitude on the part of the individual, he is rejecting the plea of the Holy Spirit and thereby sinning against the Holy Spirit. The apostle John, however, intimated that such will not take place if a person has been born of the Spirit and adopted as a child of God (1 John 3:9).

● 37-39   The writer now reinforced what he had just said by recalling the words of the prophet Isaiah (26:20 *ff.*) and the words of Habakkuk (2:3 *ff.*), and by adding the definite article *ho (ho erchomenos)* he gave the passage a messianic "application."[10] Jesus is coming again. In the meantime, the righteous ones "shall live by faith" (v. 38). There is no place for the renegade in the ranks of Christian soldiers, for "if he should draw back,/My soul has no pleasure in him" (v. 38, AT), says the Lord.

In contrast with those who "stand off" from paths of duty and devotion, the writer was confident that there still remained those who had faith "unto the saving of the soul." Perseverance has its reward for those who are faithful in their pilgrimage. They will share abundant blessings all along the way and in the end will come into possession of their heritage that is laid away for them and kept safely in heaven against that day. The fullness of salvation comes not upon earth but in heaven, and those who will enjoy heaven most will be the ones who have patiently endured and have persevered unto the end.

Notes

1. William Barclay, *The Letter to the Hebrews* (Philadelphia: The Westminster Press, 1957), p. 125.
2. Brooke Foss Westcott, *The Epistle to the Hebrews: The Greek Text with Notes and Essays* (New York: MacMillan and Company, 1889), p. 308.
3. A. T. Robertson, *Word Pictures in the New Testament*, vol. 5 (Nashville, Tenn.: Sunday School Board, SBC, 1931), p. 408.
4. Ibid., p. 408 *ff.*
5. R. Paul Caudill, *Ephesians: A Translation with Notes* (Nashville, Tenn.: Broadman Press, 1979), p. 21.
6. Robertson, p. 409.
7. Ibid., p. 412.
8. Herschel H. Hobbs, *Studies in Hebrews* (Nashville, Tenn.: Sunday School Board, SBC, 1954), p. 115.
9. Robertson, p. 416.
10. Ibid., p. 417.

CHAPTER 11

The foundation of every believer's hope is faith, and the writer to the Hebrews might well be called the great apostle of faith. No other New Testament writer dealt at such length with the subject of faith as it is found in the biblical records of the people of God in their relationship to Him under the old covenant. Indeed, faith is the scarlet thread of redemption that binds the people of God to Him and to each other.

● 1-2   In his initial word concerning the character of faith and works, the writer used an old word *hupostasis* which comes from *hupo* (under) and *histēmi* (to stand), meaning that which serves as *an underlying support* of a building, a promise, or a contract. The word came to be used in the sense of assurance *(Ménégoz)* "that steadiness of mind which holds one firm (2 Cor. 9:4)."[1] It is found in the papyri in this sense with reference to documents used to guarantee a transaction. Souter arrives at the meaning *title deed*. The writer also used the word *elegchos* which was frequently used for "proof" and subsequent "conviction." Either meaning is suitable here, and it is in the sense that the elders "had witness borne to them."

● 3-12   In his effort to affirm the "reality, the sphere, and the power of Faith,"[2] the writer turned to the historic records about the faith of the early Jewish heroes, but not until he had first expressed the primal concept of faith, namely, "that the worlds have been created by the word of God, so that what is seen has been made out of things which do not appear" (v. 3, AT). This was a devastating blow to the pagan concept of creation which held that God used existing matter to create matter whereas faith says that God made the world "out of nothing." This puts God behind everything in the universe and makes it His world while we ourselves, and everything in the world, belong to Him and are responsible to Him. God created the world directly without the use of subordinates (angelic aeons and the like), and this view of the origin of the world is fundamental to Christian faith. There were those then as now who considered matter to be eternal, but the writer's view negates that concept of the origin of the universe and places God before and behind it all.

In verse 4 the writer used a word to describe the character of the offering of Abel which leaves us with a bit of a problem. The word used is an adjective *pleiona* modifying the word *thusian* (sacrifice), and the two words together literally mean "more sacrifice." Now *pleiona* is the comparative of the word *polus*, much, and this usage of the word is found in Matthew 6:25 and Hebrews 3:3. Evidently, the Jews also found a problem in the use of the word (Gen. 4:1-15), for they developed a number of explanations concerning the preference of God for Abel's offering over that of Cain. Is it too arbitrary to assume that Abel in bringing an offering from his flock brought "the most precious thing that life supplies" to life itself: *blood?* For the Hebrews always regarded blood as *life.* "The life was the blood, and the blood was the life."[3] At any rate Abel, by his offering and "through it," (that is, *through his faith*) was witnessed to as *righteous,* and though having died "yet he keeps on speaking" (v. 4, AT). The account of his response to God by faith continues to have a message for us in today's world, for the character and impact of the works of a righteous man do not pass away.

The writer in verse 5 supplied us with another ringing example of genuine faith in his account of the translation of Enoch. The word *taken up (metetethē)* is first aorist passive indicative of *metatithēmi* which means "to transpose, to change," as in Hebrews 7:12 where the idea of change relates to the priesthood. Now the faith of Enoch is clearly seen in the fact that *before* his translation he had witness borne to him that he had been "well pleasing to God" (AT) and this would not have been possible *without faith.*

The writer in verse 6 laid down another cardinal truth about the character of faith: apart from faith in the eternal presence of God and in His disposition to become "a rewarder to those who search for Him," (AT) no one can be well pleasing *to Him* (v. 6). Faith in the existence of God, and in His ability to respond to the faith and works of humanity, is the beachhead of access to Him. Without this, there is nothing to stand on, nothing to move on from in the access pilgrimage. The supreme example of this kind of faith is found in the Hebrews as they, having received and believed in the message of Moses as God's instrument of deliverance, prepared themselves and followed him out of Egypt.

Even so, Noah (v. 7) was a man of faith, for he responded to God's revelation "concerning things not yet seen" and, acting by faith concerning the divine warning, and being "moved with reverent awe" built an ark "for the deliverance of his household" (AT). Through this act of faith he condemned the world and "became heir of the righteousness that is according to faith" (v. 7, AT). The words *being moved with reverent awe* are used to interpret a single ancient Greek word *eulabētheis* which comes from *eulabēs,* a double compound word (*eu,* well, and *labein,* to take hold carefully, in combining the two words). The resultant idea seems to indicate that Noah received the divine warning with an attitude of reverence, began to act upon it immediately, and in doing so "condemned the world," and became "heir of the righteousness that is according to faith."

In verses 8-12 the writer continued his portrayal of the faith of the patriarchs commencing with Abraham. Westcott rightly said that "With the call of Abraham the records of Faith enter on a new phase. Faith is treated henceforth in relation to a society, a people of God, through whom the divine blessings were to be extended to mankind."[4]

Abraham is often referred to as God's first missionary. God called him, he heard the call, and then he went out "not knowing whither he went." As Westcott believed, there are three aspects of Abram's faith manifested in his response to God's call: (1) "The Faith of self-surrender"; (2) "The Faith of patience"; (3) "The Faith of influence."[5] It would be difficult to conceive of a greater example of faith than that found in Abraham (v. 8). Being called to go out on a mission, he *obeyed* without knowing where he was going (v. 8). All Abraham knew was that he had been *called* of God to go on a specific mission in a land belonging to another (v. 9), and in response to that call he moved forward by faith. This he did without question, dwelling all the while "in tents, with Isaac and Jacob" who were fellow heirs of the same promise. The striking thing about Abraham was that he "kept on looking" for the city having the foundations "whose architect and builder *is* God" (v. 10, AT). The words *kept on looking* are for an old, imperfect, middle verb form *exedecheto* (from *ekdechomai*) which, as Robertson notes, is a "picturesque progressive" view of the response of Abraham whose mind and heart were set and marked by "patient waiting in spite of disappointment."[6] What is more, Sarah herself, being barren and past the normal age for the bearing of a child, "received power for the sowing of seed"

(AT) (literally, for deposit of the seed) since she had faith in God who had promised as much. She, in her response as a cosharer of Abraham on his mission, may have displayed even greater faithful obedience to God's promise.

The faith of Abraham was all the more remarkable since in his patient and obedient waiting, though "as good as dead" (v. 12), he had descendants born to him as innumerable as the stars of the heaven and as the sand along the lip of the sea (Gen. 22:17). Now these all (that is, Abraham, Sarah, and their seed) died in the faith, "not having received *{labontes}* the promises." (The text followed by Westcott and Hort uses *komisamenoi,* "to obtain," as in 10:36 and 11:39.[7]) The sense here seems to indicate that Abraham "received" the promise of the Messiah but was not privileged to live long enough to see Him face-to-face or to have the fuller revelation that has come to us concerning the Messiah. Abraham merely saw and *greeted* the promises from afar having confessed that they were "strangers and sojourners upon the earth" (AT).

● 13-16   These verses are merely a further development of the thought contained in the latter part of verse 13, namely, that the patriarchs were true men of faith, men who lived in the faith and died in the faith. They acknowledged before the world that they were on a pilgrimage and in a land in which they were "strangers and sojourners" still "seeking after a homeland" (AT). The *fatherland* from which they had come was no longer on their minds, for, if it had been so, they would have taken some of the opportunities to return. Their quest, however, was for a "better *country,* that is a heavenly one" (v. 16, AT). It was for this true fatherland for which they yearned now that they had no natural fatherland on earth and no longer yearned for such. The word *longed for* (*oregontai*) from *oregō* is an old word "for stretching out after, yearning after as in 1 Tim. 3:1."[8] God's good pleasure in the faithful response of the patriarchs was indicated by His provision for them of a divine commonwealth, a heavenly "city" which in character is both social and personal.

● 17-19   Here the writer gave us a vivid portrayal of the supreme act of testing which Abraham underwent in the offering of his son Isaac. The test consisted of two conflicts—the conflict involved with his love for his son and the obvious conflict with the previous revelation of God, for had He not said, "In Isaac shall thy seed be named" (v. 18, AT)? Nevertheless, Abraham was ready and began the process of sacrificing his only son. This he was doing "in will" and "in resolute purpose" when his hand was stayed by God. Believing in the incontrovertible character of God's promise and steadfast in his faith in spite of the apparent contradictions that loomed in his understanding of God's purpose, in his supreme act of obedience he demonstrated the character of true faith (v. 1): he followed blindly the leadership of God at each given command and trusted him fully to fulfill His every promise. In this instance, the trust lay in "Having reckoned that God is able to raise up even from the dead" (v. 19, AT). And, figuratively, this is exactly what took place; for God stayed Abraham's hand, and he received back his son. Abraham's obedience therefore "rested on his faith in the creative power of God."[9] Obviously Abraham made his decision without ambivalence, for he was ready to take an action which humanly speaking seemed to contradict the previous promise of God while his faith still rested in the confidence that God would fulfill His promise concerning the blessings that would flow into his life through Isaac and his seed. What faith! Abraham believed that God who in a miraculous manifestation of his power gave him Isaac could also raise him up "even from the dead" (v. 19). It must have been a tragic moment for Abraham, but he wavered not. His faith in God's creative power was absolute, for he made his firm decision in the full confidence that God was able to raise his son from the dead. Note the words *having reckoned (logisamenos)*, first aorist middle participle, rather than the word *reckoning, (logizamenos)*, present middle participle. In a figurative sense, Abraham did receive him back. The word *figuratively (parabolēi*, parable) occurs also in 9:9 as well as elsewhere only in the Synoptic Gospels.

● 20   The reference here is to Isaac's blessing of Jacob and Esau (Gen. 27:28-40) in which he gave the younger the highest blessing against his will, for he had preferred Esau over Jacob; but his will was overturned and his acceptance of the event "with its unseen consequences was a sign of faith."[10] The crisis was there, and Isaac apparently accepted in faith that which amounted to the inversion of the natural order which was in accord with Isaac's will. This action by Isaac, therefore, foreshadowed things to come as did the faith of Abraham who offered up his son. According to natural law, had Abraham offered his son it would have been the end of things for his seed. So did the death of Christ, in the eyes of many, spell out the defeat of His mission and purpose as God's only Son.

● 21   The blessing of Jacob and the blessing of Isaac offered a new turn in the fulfillment of God's holy purpose, namely, His special blessing rested not merely upon a particular son but upon all the sons of Joseph. They were all to share in the fulfillment of God's redemptive purpose. Likewise the preference shown Joseph over Reuben, the older brother, harks back to the case of Jacob where the younger is preferred over the elder, and, thereby, for all "practical purposes," gave Joseph precedence over Reuben in "the fulfillment of a righteous judgment in the providence of God."[11]

● 22   The faith of Joseph is obvious and marked a further stage in God's redemptive purpose. He and his brothers, notwithstanding their prosperity, had to look for something beyond the present. Egypt was not to be their dwelling place, and they must never lose sight of their destiny in which he himself, figuratively, would participate. He remembered God's promise to Abraham, and the sons of Israel carried out his charge (Ex. 13:19; Josh. 24:32).

In verses 23-31 the faith, as Westcott observed, which had hitherto been regarded "under the discipline of patience and sacrifice," now appears on the stage of action.[12] The action centers first in Moses (23-28) and second in the people led by him on their divinely appointed pilgrimage (29-31).

● 23-28   When Moses was born he was hid by his parents for three months because he was *well formed* and beautiful, possessing both bodily grace and charm (*asteion*, from *astu*, city "of the city"). Literally, "the child was goodly" (Robertson). What is more, the parents of Moses were fearless of the king's edict.

When Moses grew up, he demonstrated his own faith by his refusal to be called "the son of Pharaoh's daughter" (v. 24). The word *refused* (*ērnēsato*, first aorist middle indicative of *arneomai*) means "to deny, to refuse." The pleasures of the palace and the lavish splendors of Pharaoh's life-style—and that of his household—failed to affect Moses who chose rather "to suffer together with the people of God than to have temporary pleasure of sin" (v. 25). Moses' choice was self-made (second aorist middle of the verb *haireō, to take for oneself a position*) (Robertson), and his desire to share in the fellowship of his people's sufferings foreshadowed the passionate longings of the apostle Paul to experience "the fellowship" of Christ's sufferings (Phil. 3:10). No one of the Israelites pushed Moses into this position. He was moved by the Spirit of God and by his own will under God's leading.

In verses 27-28 there is a bold portrayal of the vision of Moses. He "kept on looking away unto the reward" (v. 26)—the reward bound up in God's redemptive mission which embraced, as another stage in the development of

God's purpose, the entrance into the Land of Promise. After all, the pleasure of sin is but temporary, and all that the Egyptian court might have offered him in the way of carnal pleasures would have been but for the moment. The reward for which Moses was looking, while not defined, consisted of more than the realization of the entrance into the Promised Land in Canaan by the children of God. A glimpse of the character of the reward is found in 1 Corinthians 2:9. Whether the leaving of Egypt had to do with his flight to Midian or to the Exodus matters not at all; for it was by his faith, a faith that delivered him from fear of the king's wrath, that it all took place. And he endured because his faith was "the title deed of things hoped for, a conviction about things not seen" (v. 1); "for, as seeing Him who is invisible, he endured."

Moses was conscious of his relationship to the redemptive purpose of God and boldly acknowledged that relationship. This is why he "kept the passover and the sprinkling of the blood." He had faith that if he followed God's command in this act of sacrifice, God was able to save the firstborn of His people from the hand of the destroyer. It is easy for one to see in the celebration of this first Passover that the sacrifice of the lamb and the sprinkling of the blood was a type of the sacrifice of Christ in the shedding of His blood before all the people, thereby becoming the Mediator for perfect access to God on the part of the whole world of men who might come to Him by faith. Likewise, the celebration of the Passover remains as a witness to the deliverance of the Hebrew children from Egypt even as the observance of the Lord's Supper is a memorial to His atoning act as the great High Priest in behalf of all people.

● 29   Here the faith of the people matched the faith of Moses their leader in triumphantly crossing the Red Sea "as by dry land." Notice the writer's words concerning the Egyptians who, not "by faith," but "taking trial," were *swallowed up* (first aorist passive indicative of the old verb *katapinō*, to drink down, to swallow down, Matt. 23:24). They made a trial of their own power, tugging at their own bootstraps, and they failed pathetically as people always fail when rashly assaulting the issues of life apart from the redeeming purpose of God.

● 30-31   Even so, the people, following in the footsteps of their leaders, encircled the walls of Jericho for seven days and overthrew those same walls "by faith." It was a wearying, painful experience but nothing to be compared with the triumph of their faith which became symbolic of the victory of the church

(Matt. 16:18). Here, for the first time in the biblical account of the redemptive mission of God through the Israelites, a stranger to Israel is received into the circle of God's people. Rahab, the harlot, "perished not" with the other children of disobedience because she welcomed the Hebrew spies with peace as guests in her own house.

● 32-38   The writer turned to a brief discussion of faith as it was reflected in the life of the Hebrew nation. In recounting the colorful history of the Israelites beginning with the call of Abraham and extending to the occupation of the Promised Land, the writer gave detailed examples of faith operating in the lives of God's people. He provided a brief roll call of a number of the great heroes of the past without a detailed record of their achievement.

The writer was apparently "embarrassed" (Robertson) because of his inability to do justice to the deeds and the sufferings of these valiant leaders of the past. Naming only six of the heroes (Gideon, Barak, Samson, Jephthah, David, Samuel), he merely mentioned "the prophets."

The writer again emphasized (vv. 33-35a) the role of faith on the part of these courageous leaders, describing in part their typical victories as they "through faith conquered kingdoms, brought about righteousness, obtained promises, shut the mouths of lions." In the midst of the numerous violent assaults of human origin, there came to them strength that made them able to face the crises in triumph and even to become "powerful in war." It is interesting to note that women were also "tortured" and some of them received back "their dead by a resurrection" (35).

The writer next described the intense sufferings and grave trials of those who were of the faith. The various categories of suffering are frightening to contemplate: "derisive tortures," scourgings, imprisonment (v. 36); stoning, bodily dismemberment, sword slaughter, wandering about "in sheep skins, in goat skins, being needy, afflicted, ill treated" (v. 37); wandering about and dwelling in deserts, mountains, caves, and in "the holes of the earth" (v. 38). And at the heart of their faith was the resurrection hope—"that they might obtain a better resurrection" (v. 35). The words *of whom the world was not worthy* appear to indicate that the suffering Christians were "men worth more than the whole world, and they lacked all."[13]

● 39   Notwithstanding the unwavering faith and the unflinching courage of these mighty heroes of faith, they "received not the promise" (v. 39)—that is, the complete fulfillment of the messianic promise—for their trials and suffering would give way to a complete realization of the messianic kingdom. They had, of course, experienced the fulfillment of many individual special promises (as in 11:33).

● 40   The "something better" (v. 40) is bound up in the "better promises" (8:6) which involved the foresight of God in His glorious and gracious purpose for all the saints. The final, victorious joys of believers will come only at the time of the Savior's final triumph when "he shall deliver the kingdom to the God and Father, whenever he shall abolish all rule and all authority and power. For he must reign until he put all the enemies under his feet. Then the death, the last enemy, is done away with."[14] The state of perfection comes at that time and will not be realized by individual groups "apart from us" while in the flesh.

Notes

1. A. T. Robertson, *Word Pictures in the New Testament,* vol. 5 (Nashville, Tenn.: Sunday School Board, SBC, 1931), p. 418.

2. Brooke Foss Westcott, *The Epistle to the Hebrews: The Greek Text with Notes and Essays* (New York: MacMillan and Company, 1889), p. 351.

3. William Barclay, *The Letter to the Hebrews* (Philadelphia: The Westminster Press, 1957), p. 148.

4. Westcott, p. 359.

5. Ibid., p. 357 *ff.*

6. Robertson, p. 422.

7. Brooke Foss Westcott and Fenton John Anthony Hort, *The New Testament in the Original Greek* (New York: The MacMillan Company, 1929), *in loco.*

8. Robertson, p. 424.

9. Westcott, p. 368.

10. Ibid., p. 370.

11. Ibid.

12. Ibid., p. 372.

13. Ibid., p. 383.

14. R. Paul Caudill, *First Corinthians: A Translation with Notes* (Nashville, Tenn.: Broadman Press, 1983), p. 98.

CHAPTER 12

As Dr. A. T. Robertson noted, the chapter divisions here are unfortunate since 12:1-3 constitutes a logical climax to the argument advanced (10:19 to 12:3) concerning the "better promises" (8:6) along with a stirring appeal for "loyalty to Christ."[1] In verse 1 the continuity of the argument is indicated by the triple compound inferential particle (*toigaroun*), used to introduce an inference, as "for that very reason, then, therefore" (Bauer). The word, used only here and in 1 Thessalonians 4:8, indicates concluding emphasis.

● 1   In verses 1-13 the emphasis has to do with discipline. Hebrew Christians should be motiviated on their pilgrimage by the loyalty of the great throng of "witnesses" with which they are surrounded. The picture is that of an amphitheater with its *arena* and the "tiers upon tiers of seats rising up like a cloud."[2] And the *witnesses* (*marturōn,* from which we get our word *martyr*) are the heroes of faith that have gone before. They have run their race and now are looking down upon those who follow in their train. They are more than mere spectators (*theatai*); they are witnesses who have had their own experience on the Christian pilgrimage and are testifying to that experience. Motivated by their presence, Hebrew Christians are to divest themselves, as a Christian runner on life's pilgrimage, of everything that might impede their mission. Like the athletes in the stadium who are out to win their race, the Christian is to lay aside "every weight and the easily ensnaring sin." This refers not merely to material things that the runner must lay aside but also to handicaps like "doubt, pride, sloth, anything."[3] In view of the emphasis placed on apostasy by the writer, it appears that he had this problem especially in mind as he wrote, for there were many Hebrew Christians who had made their profession of faith, but had apparently failed to make worthy progress in the role they had to play as

163

"fellow soldiers" in Christ's redemptive mission. Moreover, they were to run with patience the race, a race that is "set before us" by the divine purpose of God.

● 2-3   While there is motivation and inspiration in the thoughts concerning the "throng of witnesses" looking down upon the amphitheater in which Christians run their race, the greatest motivation lies in the example of Jesus "the founder and perfecter of the faith." He is the One whom pilgrims should fix their eyes and mind upon, recalling how "in place of the joy that was set before Him" He voluntarily went on to the cross in one supreme act of sacrifice as the true Lamb of God, despising the shameful atmosphere that accompanied His death, and "sat down" in His royal place of honor and majesty at the right hand of God's throne. Christ *did not have to* undergo the humiliation and the shame of the cross which was the instrument of death for only the meanest of criminals, but He voluntarily chose the death route of the cross in place of the joy that He was soon to realize in the glorious triumph marked by His resurrection from the dead and ascension on high. This was the joy that was "set before Him" as He contemplated the merciless pangs of Golgotha. The verb used for *has sat down* (*kekathiken*) is perfect active indicative of *kathizo* and means that while the action took place in the past, He is *still there* (1:3).

● 4   If the Hebrew Christians felt that they had been the subject of grave hostility directed against them by nonbelievers, let them consider Christ as their example, for He is the "standard of comparison."[4] After all, they had not yet "resisted unto blood" (v. 4). Their struggle had not been a mortal one, costing their life, as was true in the case of Jesus. Therefore, they were not to give way to weariness and become *tired out* in their souls, for conflict with sin is an unending struggle for the Christian on earth.

● 5-6   The writer chided the Hebrew Christians for forgetting the exhortations spoken to them by the Lord as a father would speak to a son (see Prov. 5:11-12 and Rev. 3:19). Evidently they had regarded lightly the Lord's instruction concerning the discipline that comes to every one including the children of God. After all, discipline is to be expected from God on the part of the children whom He loves (v. 6). The word translated *disciplines* is from an old verb (*mastigoi,* from *mastix,* lash, whip). The writer might have referred the Hebrews to Matthew 5:7 which portrays graphically the disciplines of Christ in His sufferings.

• 7   In seasons of discipline, no matter how severe, and though others might flee in the face of such sufferings, Christians are to hold out, and stand their ground, and keep on waiting for the ultimate fulfillment of God's promises to them.

Furthermore, Christians are to remember the early Roman household in which the father had the supreme power—even of life and death. The father's power in Rome (*patria potestas*) was by Roman law an absolute thing. Whether the son remained single or married, the power of the father was supreme. If he desired to do so, he could scourge his son or sell him into slavery or put him to death; this latter right was exercised until the days of Augustus. The Hebrews are rather to think of the disciplines they suffer through the permissive will of God as something that equips them with strength and inspiration for advancement toward the realization of the full purposes of God for themselves and for all humanity.

• 8   To be without the chastening hand of discipline whereof all of the followers of Christ "have been made partakers" amounts to placing one into the category of illegitimacy which disclaims their true sonship in the heavenly family.

• 9   Here the writer focused on some of the characteristics "of earthly and heavenly discipline."[5] Among the ancient Romans, the son was forever subject to the will of his father. Most likely all the readers were familiar with the *patria potestas* under which rule the son lived in subjection to his father's power while the father lived. Perhaps parental discipline was never more severe than that in the Roman household. The Hebrews also had parental discipline though not so severe as that of the Romans. But surely all of the readers understood the writer's words *fathers of our flesh as disciplinarians,* and how the children "continued to respect" their fathers. From this established fact, and with greater reason and more convincing force, the children of the Heavenly Father could understand how they should rather be much more "in subjection to the Father of our spirits" (v. 9). And why? For the simple reason that the discipline of God leads to a greater end, for by submission to the discipline of the Heavenly Father, His children "live!" The discipline of earthly parents is a transitory matter and has its limitations because of our earthly nature. In our complete subjection to the discipline of God, our response enjoys the highest blessing, the blessing of life (*kai zēsomen,* "and we shall live"). God offers this life freely to us, but we must respond faithfully to God's promise to enjoy it.

● 10   Moreover, the chastening of earthly fathers was based upon what seemed "best to them," but the chastening of our Heavenly Father is always "for *our* benefit." The human method of discipline, therefore, is inferior to the discipline of God just as "the claims of the one are inferior to the claims of the other."[6] Furthermore, the discipline of earthly parents may be selfishly inclined but not so of divine discipline. God's goal is always for the benefit of His children. And while discipline of the earthly parent relates only to the transitory aspect of human life, the discipline of the Heavenly Father corresponds in its purpose and design to His eternal redemptive nature.

● 11   But there is a general principle that is operative with regard to all discipline whether human or divine: all discipline, for the time being, appears to be grievous rather than joyous (v. 11), but for the Christian the issue of the conflict afterward finds expression in the "peaceable fruit of righteousness" in those who are "trained by it." "The fruit of righteousness," of course, means fruit that is righteous in character. The word *exercised (gegumnasmenois)* summons before the eye the activity of a gymnasium.

● 12-13   In view of the necessity for discipline which is painful as well as necessary, the writer begged his readers to make the most of the divine disciplines of life that they encounter daily and harks back to the Old Testament for imagery. (See Isa. 35:3.) The figures of "hands" and "knees" and "feet" relate to the strength and powers necessary for the progressive realization of God's purpose on the holy, redemptive pilgrimage of which they are a part in Christ Jesus. The figure *drooping hands,* used here in the perfect passive participle, indicates "listless, weakened, slackened, weary, drooping" hands. The figure *weakened knees* is used of the paralytic in Luke 5:24. If there are external doings in the way of progress, let them be removed "that the limbs of the lame be not dislocated" (v. 13). The Christian pilgrim is to have loving concern for the journeying of others, always having their welfare and their progress at heart.

● 14-15   The Hebrews are to endeavor to maintain a peaceful relationship with all and to strive "for holiness," knowing that apart from holiness "no one will see the Lord." These verses reflect in a beautiful way the spirit and the mood of Jesus' first sermon delivered in his home synagogue of Nazareth. "Give peace a chase as if in a hunt,"[7] and this *chase* is to relate to all people (v. 15). Special care is to be given to the probability of someone who is in need of "the grace of God"

(v. 15). And the Christians are to see that no quarter is given to "any root of bitterness" that, "springing up," may bring trouble and cause someone to be "defiled" (*mianthōsin,* from *miainō,* an old verb "to dye, to stain, to defile."[8] See Titus 1:15. Sin is a terrible thing with the sweeping and destructive character of a wildfire.

● 16   Some commentators raise the question as to whether the word *fornicator* like the word *profane* relates to Esau who "for a single meal gave up his own birthright." We prefer to regard the two words as separate in their relationships to the rest of the writer's emphasis. The emphasis of the writer appears to center on the person himself who by personal impurity may be a stumbling block and failure in God's sight. For instance one who blatantly disregards God's blessings, as did Esau, may also be a stumbling block to the redemptive mission of God. Esau bartered recklessly for moments of sensory pleasure his birthright which afforded him, by divinely intended prerogative, a unique role in God's mission for Israel. (See Deut. 21:17 and also 1 Chron. 5:1 with reference to the "double portion" of the firstborn. See also the warning in Deut. 8:8-14.)

● 17   The issue in verse 17 is not that of salvation (*sotēria*). After Esau had given up his birthright for a single meal to satisfy his carnal desires, he apparently reviewed his action and afterward desired to inherit the blessing, but was rejected. He found "no place for a change of mind" in his father Isaac although he tearfully sought it. He had willfully committed a tragic sin, and there was no second chance (Heb. 6:6; 10:26). Esau was *still* his father's son, but he lost his place in the royal line of blessing because of his sin. The writer would have the example of Esau serve as a warning to any of the Hebrew Christians who might be tempted to stand off and turn away from their divine responsibilities in God's redemptive mission.

In bringing to a close the main argument that runs throughout the epistle, the writer presented a graphic picture (vv. 18-29) of the two covenants in contrast: On the one hand, there is grace while on the other hand there is terror. The crux of the writer's emphasis is the relationship of privilege to responsibility: "Greater privileges bring greater responsibility."[9]

● 18-21   The writer contrasted the relative positions of the Israelites, when God gave to them through Moses at Mount Sinai the law, with that of the Hebrew Christians and their relation to God's divine purpose of worldwide redemption. At the giving of the law, the scene at Sinai was marked by frightful foreboding. There were fire, and darkness, and gloom, and tempests, and the sound of the trumpet (vv. 18-19). Even the mountain itself was all but lost to view midst the fire and the smoke which symbolized the divine Presence. The whole situation was palpable, yet so forbidding that none of the Jews dared to draw near; and even if a beast should "touch the mountain," it was to be stoned (v. 20). And Moses himself, moved by the frightful manifestation declared, "I am terrified and trembling" (v. 21).

● 22-23   Now the scene changes, and the contrast is vivid. No longer are the Christians faced with the terrors of Sinai, for they themselves have access to the heavenly Presence. There is no terror and no disturbing material circumstances that provoke fear, for Christian revelation is come, and in its fulfillment there is access to God for all who would come by faith. Paul showed in striking contrast Mount Sinai (the present Jerusalem) with the heavenly Jerusalem which is above (Gal. 4:21-31). Here heaven is termed "a spiritual mountain and city" (Robertson) and there are "myriads of angels in festal gatherings" (v. 22) which mark the joyful character of heaven. The expression *to the assembly of the firstborn who are enrolled in heaven* apparently refers, in a general sense, to all the redeemed as in Matthew 16:18, Colossians 1:18, Ephesians 5:24-32, and is "equivalent to the kingdom of God."[10] The Christians, though yet on earth, are already enrolled in heaven (Luke 10:20; Phil. 3:20; 4:3; Rev. 13:8). And the Christians are to remember that they have also come "to God the Judge of all" as well as to "the spirits of righteous ones made perfect" (*teteleiōmenōn,* v. 23).

● 24   Those who are in Christ are able, personally, to draw near unto Him. The writer also reminded the Hebrew Christians again of the fact that Jesus is "the mediator of a new covenant" and of "the blood of sprinkling that speaks better than *that of* Abel" (v. 24). Jesus is placed in contrast with Moses who served as mediator of the first covenant in that he led the children of Israel out of their bondage in Egypt. And His blood offering speaks better than *that of* Abel. This "New Covenant" of which Jesus is the Mediator, however, is *new* both in time and in character. Abel's blood of course still speaks (11:4), but its message was only a harbinger of the "blood of sprinkling" of which Jesus is the Mediator. Moreover, the blood of Abel brought down the wrath of God upon the heart and life of Cain; but the blood of Christ brings down "forgiveness and speaks peace to man."[11] How great the difference!

● 25-27   These verses emphasize, in added measure, the inescapable responsibilities of Christians. Already the stirring contrast between the position of the Israelites and the Christians and their respective responses to God's redemptive purpose has been clearly presented. Now the writer turned to the Christians in a final word of admonition concerning the final revelation (vv. 25-27). The Christians are reminded of the dire consequences of the Israelites who "rejected the One warning them on earth" (v. 25) and are reminded of the fact that Christians who turn themselves away from the warning that comes from heaven have even less of a chance to escape. Quoting from Haggai 2:6, the writer pointed vividly to the cosmic catastrophe that "once more" will cause to tremble both earth and heaven (v. 27). But in the midst of it all, the Christian is to know that God's kingdom will *not* be shaken, for it is eternal.

● 28-29   Herein lies the basis for the Christian's loyalty to Christ and for his "calm trust in God" (Robertson). He is a part of God's kingdom which is unshakable. The words *let us keep on (echōmen)*, which we have regarded as volitive, might be regarded as a futuristic subjunctive as in 8:3 (*ho prosenegkēi*). The point is, the Christian is to keep on keeping on—both with reference to getting the needed grace and the matter of *serving God* worthily—and that with "reverence and awe."

After all, our God is not only a God of grace; He is also "a consuming fire" (v. 29). See 10:31.

Notes

1. A. T. Robertson, *(Word Pictures in the New Testament,* vol. 5 (Nashville, Tenn.: Sunday School Board, SBC, 1931), p. 432.

2. Ibid.

3. Ibid.

4. William Barclay, *The Letter to the Hebrews* (Philadelphia: The Westminster Press, 1957), p. 197.

5. Brooke Foss Westcott, *The Epistle to the Hebrews: The Greek Text with Notes and Essays* (New York: MacMillan and Company, 1889), p. 401-403.

6. Ibid., p. 405.

7. Robertson, p. 437.
8. Ibid., p. 437 *ff.*
9. Westcott, p. 411.
10. Robertson, p. 440.
11. Westcott, p. 419.

CHAPTER 13

Some regard chapter 13 of Hebrews as a sort of postscript or appendix. It is true that chapters 1—12 constitute a perfect entity; but as one reviews the contents of the chapter as a whole, it does not appear to be separate, self-contained, or independent. The chapter, when carefully reviewed, appears to support logically the premise of chapters 1—12. In the turn of emphasis with which the chapter begins, the writer dealt first with some Christian social duties (1—6). The nature of the admonitions in these verses may indicate (Westcott) that they were slanted to church members who were wealthy and influential. Whatever be the case, the precepts are relevant and represent much-needed aspects of interpersonal Christian relations.

● 1   Brotherly love is an absolute necessity. Without this mark of character, no one can imitate Christ. Love, like the bond of faith, should be universal. It is interesting to note that our English word *Philadelphia* is merely a transliteration of this same Greek word *(philadelphia)*.

● 2   Particular loving concern should be manifested toward strangers, for it is possible thereby, said the writer, for one to entertain angels without knowing it. The reference is obviously to Genesis 18 and 19 where Sarah and Abraham did this.

● 3   Christians are not to lose sight of those in bonds, but rather are to think of themselves "as bound with them." It was a common thing in that day for Christians to be put in prison for their debts—in spite of their poverty. Some were put in the mines or banished to an island or imprisoned for nothing more than their loyalty to Christ and to His church. The bond of sympathy should always be manifest to the suffering and mistreated ones. The response of early Christians to their brothers in this respect was so marked that Emperor

Licinius had legislation passed that " 'no one was to show kindness to sufferers in prison by supplying them with food, and that no one was to show mercy to those starving in prison.' "[1]

● 4   Some ascetics of the day who looked down upon marriage went so far as to castrate themselves in the hope of attaining greater purity.[2] Others went to the other extreme of sexual immorality. In the face of this, the writer reminded the Hebrews that the marriage bed is to remain undefiled—that is, there is to be no adultery associated with it; and all are to remember that both the fornicators and adulterers will be judged by God.

● 5-6   The life-style of the Christian is to be "free from the love of money." The love of money is the root of all kinds of evil, and for this reason the Christian is never to fall prey to inordinate regard for material things. Rather, the Christian is to remember God's promise: "I will never desert you, neither will I ever forsake you." God's presence is as constant as the days of the believer who lives each day by faith. In further justification of this mood of confidence which the Christian is to maintain, the writer quoted from Psalm 118:6. The word *to me (emoi)* is an ethical dative used with the word *helper (boēthos)* which is an old adjective that carries the idea of one running to the cry of another to help in time of need.

In verses 7-17 the writer both warned and admonished Christians concerning their regard for their religious leaders, past and present, and their response to religious duties in general.

● 7   Already the writer had called to mind many of the heroes of the faith (ch. 11), and now he admonished the Christians to keep in mind these leaders— their lifestyles and their faith which they were to imitate. The reference is not so much to special actions as it is to the spirit of their lives and the manner in which they responded to God's mission for them. Particularly the faith of these leaders is to be recalled, and imitated, for it was their unshakable faith that gave them access to the triumphal victories they enjoyed.

● 8   The leader of all the leaders of the churches is Jesus Christ, and He is the same "yesterday, and today and forever." His high priesthood is to have no successor, and His blood offering was once and for all. His role as Lamb of God is unchangeable.

● 9   Strange and diverse teachings were to be found on every hand and the Hebrews were constantly in danger of being drawn away from their mission as followers of Christ by these novel and often times attractive views. Nothing was to be gained by falling prey to the fascinating teachings to which they were constantly subjected. Stability to the mind and heart could only come by the grace of God which at heart is the free and undeserved manifestation of God's redemptive love experienced by believers. Westcott defined this grace as "the free outflow of divine love for the quickening and support of man."[3] Only God's grace is capable of sustaining both mind and heart in the face of the "windy" theories concerning religious matters that abound so much today as they did then. With the Hebrews, there was the temptation to lean upon Jewish ritualism and formalism which in themselves were incapable of bringing the needed strength to the spiritual life.

● 10-13   Here again the contrast between the Levitical ritual of sacrifice and the sacrifice of Jesus on the cross whereby He might "sanctify the people through His own blood" is crystal clear. For instance, those who served the tabernacle could not eat of the offering, for the bodies of the sacrificial animals of the Levitical system, whose blood was brought into the holy place by the high priest *as a sacrifice,* were "burned outside the camp." On the other hand, the Christian has only one sacrifice—Christ Himself upon the cross and that "outside the camp" (v. 11)—and in this sacrifice the Christian participates, for Christ becomes our sustenance.

The parallel between the Levitical sacrifice ritual of the Old Testament and that of Jesus, the better sacrifice (v. 13), as previously discussed (9:13 to 10:18), is even more clearly marked.

Here again the issue is clear, and the challenge unmistakable: Christians are to "withdraw from Judaism even in its first and purest shape. It had been designed by God as a provisional system, and its work was done."[4] The sacrificial ritual of Judaism must be abandoned in its entirety, and the followers of Jesus are to "keep on going out there to Him, outside the camp, bearing His reproach" (v. 13). The only place for the Christian to stand is beside the cross ("outside the camp") which Jesus endured "despising shame" (12:2). Even so, Moses turned his back upon "the treasures of Egypt" (11:26).

● 14   The fullness of the spiritual heritage of Christians was not to be found in the provisional system whose work, though designed by God, was done. The old order was transitory and offered no refuge as an abiding city; rather, Christians, turning away from the old sacrificial system for the work of the great

High Priest who is Jesus, are to "keep on striving for the One that is to come."

● 15   Jesus is both our High Priest and our Sacrifice, and it is through Him *(di' autou)*, and not through another, that we are to *"keep on offering up* a sacrifice of praise continually to God"—which was interpreted by the writer as the fruit of lips that praise His name. (See Ps. 50:14 and Lev. 7:12.)

● 16   This sacrifice of praise (spiritual sacrifice), however, is to be accompanied with "the doing of good and sharing." The ancient word *eupoiias,* "the doing of good," is "The general word for kindly service"[5] and followed by the old word *koinōnias* (fellowship, sharing) would seem to indicate, in the combined form, help in the form of alms.

● 17   The writer now looked back to church leaders, as in verse 7, whom he had charged the Hebrews to remember and imitate. He charged the Hebrews to "submit *to them,*" for as good shepherds these leaders were aware of their responsibilities to "keep watch" over the flock and often in doing so were sleepless *(agrupnousin,* from *agreō,* to search, and *hupnos,* sleep, to search for sleep).

● 18-19   The closing verses of the epistle are filled with "words of personal solicitude and tenderness."[6] First, the writer urged his readers for continued prayer in his behalf and that of his fellow workers. The plural *us* as used here, and subsequently, suggests that the writer has in mind those who shared with him in his immediate witness. Some think that the writer and his co-workers may have fallen under the criticism of others, and perhaps that is why he said "we are persuaded that we have a good conscience, desiring to conduct ourselves commendably in all things" (v. 18). If the conscience is not good *(kalēn),* it may lead one astray. To be good, it must have Christian instruction and divine motivation. The use of the words *restored to you soon* (v. 19) are unclear as to exact meaning. Was the writer ill at the time, in prison, or not physically well enough to travel? Who but the Heavenly Father knows? At any rate, there was obviously a longing to see his friends.

● 20-22   Having asked his readers to pray for him and his co-workers, the writer then prayed for his readers. The words, taken together, form a benediction that is surpassingly beautiful and meaningful to Christians. Beginning with the words *the God of the peace,* a typical expression in the Pauline Epistles, the writer focused on the resurrection of Jesus "from the realm of the dead" (the only direct mention of the resurrection in the epistle, though implied reference is found elsewhere as in 1:3). The writer prayerfully hoped that God would make the readers complete (*katartisai,* from *katartizō, to equip,* as in 10:5) "in every good thing to do His will, doing in us [that is, working in us] that which is well pleasing in His sight, through Jesus Christ; to whom *be* the glory for ever" (v. 21). This is all that matters in the life-style of believers (John 6:38). In reviewing what he had written, the writer spoke apologetically of the brevity with which he had dealt with the themes he had touched upon in the letter.

● 23 He wanted them to know that Timothy "has been set free" (maybe from prison in Rome, if he came at Paul's request—2 Tim. 4:11,21), and of the possibility of their seeing him and Timothy together soon.

● 24 The words *they of Italy* may refer to Italian Christians who were at the time in company of the writer, or they may refer to those who, from Italy, send their greetings.

● 25 The writer closed the epistle with the greeting found in Titus 3:15. Here, as in the final greetings of the Epistles of Paul, is the obvious desire for those receiving the epistle to experience the glorious grace of God.

Notes

1. William Barclay, *The Letter to the Hebrews* (Philadelphia: The Westminster Press, 1957), p. 220.
2. Ibid., p. 221.
3. Brooke Foss Westcott, *The Epistle to the Hebrews: The Greek Text with Notes and Essays* (New York: MacMillan and Company, 1889), p. 438.
4. Ibid., p. 444.
5. Ibid., p. 446.
6. Ibid., p. 447.